Albufeira Travel Gui Itinerary

Image 1 - View from the pier to the Fisherman's Beach - Praia dos Pescadores

Welcome to Albufeira, the sparkling jewel of Portugal's Algarve region. Over the years, Albufeira has woven a magic of its own, standing as a mesmerizing blend of quaint charm and vibrant energy, becoming a go-to destination for travelers seeking sun-soaked beaches, fascinating culture, and warm hospitality.

This comprehensive travel guide aims to provide you with all the essential information needed to plan your unforgettable trip to Albufeira. Whether you're embarking on a solo journey, planning a family holiday, or dreaming of a romantic getaway, this guide will ensure that you make the most of what this beautiful Portuguese town has to offer.

About the Guide

Designed to act as your personal travel companion, this guide provides extensive details about Albufeira's transport facilities, accommodations for all budgets, must-see landmarks, activities for thrill-seekers, food havens, and unique cultural experiences.

Moreover, it includes an essential information section to prepare you for any circumstance, tips for sustainable travel, and insights on day trips from Albufeira.

Contents

Albufeira Travel Guide with 3-day Itinerary 1

1. Introduction 6
    About Albufeira 7
    Albufeira's History and Culture 7
    A Glimpse into Albufeira's Past 7
    Albufeira's Cultural Identity 8
    The Influence of Tourism and Modernity..8

2. Getting to Albufeira 11
    By train..11
    By bus 11
    By Air 12
    From Faro Airport to Albufeira 13
    Useful Telephone Numbers and Travel Information 17

3. Getting Around Albufeira..19
    - 3.1 Public Transportation 19
    - 3.2 Car Rentals 19
    - 3.3 Bikes and Scooters 20
    - 3.4 Walking..20

4. Accommodation...21
    4.1 Best Areas to Stay in Albufeira 21
    4.1 Luxury Hotels..23

- 4.2 Mid-range Hotels 27
- 4.3 Budget Options 29
- 4.4 ApartHotels 31
- 4.5 Our Top Hotel Suggestion 32
- 5. Sightseeing in Albufeira 34
  - 5.1 Historical Landmarks 34
  - 5.2 Beaches 37
  - 5.3 Nature and Parks 38
  - 5.4 Museums and Galleries 38
  - 5.5 Religious Sites 39
- 6. Activities and Experiences 41
  - 6.1 Water Sports 41
  - 6.2 Golf Courses 42
  - 6.3 Hiking and Cycling Trails 43
  - 6.4 Nightlife 43
  - 6.5 Family Friendly Activities 44
  - 6.6 Spa and Wellness Centers 45
- 7. Dining and Cuisine 47
  - 7.1 Portuguese Cuisine 47
  - 7.2 Seafood in Albufeira 56
  - 7.3 Vegetarian and Vegan Options 57
  - 7.4 Street Food and Snacks 58
  - 7.5 Wine and Spirits 59
  - 7.6 Dining Etiquette in Albufeira 60
  - 7.7 Top Rated Restaurants 62
- 8. Shopping in Albufeira 64
  - 8.1 Shopping Centers and Malls 64

- 8.2 Local Markets 64
- 8.3 Specialty and Gift Shops 64
- 8.4 Buying Souvenirs 65
- 8.5 Portuguese Crafts and Textiles 65

9. Seasonal Events and Festivals 67
- 9.1 Music Festivals 67
- 9.2 Traditional Portuguese Festivals 67
- 9.3 Sports Events 68
- 9.4 Art and Film Festivals 68

10. Essential Information 70
- 10.1 Safety and Security 70
- 10.2 Health and Medical Services 70
- 10.3 Money and Banking 70
- 10.4 Local Laws and Customs 70
- 10.5 Useful Phrases and Language Tips 70
- 10.6 Weather and Clothing Tips 75
- 10.7 Frequently Asked Questions 76
- 10.8 Top Things to do in Albufeira 80
- 10.9 The Best Tours to Book in Albufeira 81

11. Day Trips from Albufeira 82
- 11.1 Lagos 82
- 11.2 Faro 84
- 11.3 Tavira 87
- 11.4 Silves 89
- 11.5 Loulé 91

3-Day Travel Itinerary to Albufeira 95
- 1st Day in Albufeira 95

1st Day in Albufeira – Day Map 106
2nd Day in Albufeira 107
2nd Day in Albufeira – Day Map 117
3rd Day in Albufeira 119
3rd Day in Albufeira – Day Map 122
Thank you! 123

1. Introduction

Albufeira is a city in the south of Portugal, from the region of Algarve. It belongs to the Faro district. It is mainly a tourist destination, due to its coastal conditions, an excellent climate - especially in the summer - and active nightlife. Because of this, Albufeira expands to approximately 300,000 residents during its peak months and during New Year celebrations. During the rest of the year, many restaurants and bars or nightclubs close, due to low activity and city movement. So, if you're planning on making your trip to Albufeira between May and September, don't forget to pack fresh and loose clothes, swimming suit, hats, comfortable sneakers and certainly lots of sunscreen. Also, remember to hydrate regularly during all of the activities you eventually choose to pursue.

Lunchtime in Portugal starts at around 1pm. As for dinnertime, it generally begins at about 9pm. Just as a comparison, Portugal's neighbors – the Spanish – have their meals way later. But both countries share a common trait – their pleasure for long meals and sitting around the table after eating for hours. Don't find it strange if you see people still eating at 6pm – it's because after lunch, between conversations and drinks, there will probably get to a point when hunger strikes again!

It also may be useful to let you know that in Portugal tipping is not mandatory and definitely not included in the receipt and final cost of the meal. It is a somewhat common practice to leave something after you pay, usually 2 or 3 euros, but rarely does anyone give more than that. Furthermore, no one will look at you differently or think it's strange if you don't leave a tip.

About Albufeira

Albufeira, once a humble fishing village, has blossomed into one of the most alluring holiday destinations in Portugal. It's renowned for its stunning beaches framed by ochre cliffs, bustling nightlife, and a historic old town brimming with pastel-colored houses and ancient Moorish influences. Its charm lies in its capability to provide a multifaceted experience – from peaceful beach afternoons and enlightening cultural explorations to thrilling water sports and vibrant night markets.

Albufeira's History and Culture

Albufeira, a captivating town on the southern coast of Portugal in the Algarve region, has a history as rich and colorful as the town itself. This town, which is now synonymous with golden beaches, azure waters, and lively tourism, has a past that stretches back over thousands of years and has seen various cultures settle in its bounds, each leaving an indelible mark on the land and the community. To truly appreciate Albufeira's allure, we must first delve into its past and explore its cultural heritage.

A Glimpse into Albufeira's Past

Albufeira's history is long and complex, beginning with prehistoric settlers who left their mark in the form of Neolithic burial mounds known as "antas." The earliest known inhabitants of the area were the Celtic tribes, who settled there around the 8th century BCE. Yet, the first substantial influences on Albufeira came from the Romans.

The Romans arrived in the 2nd century BCE and named the city Baltum. They built roads, bridges, and aqueducts, leaving a profound impact on Albufeira. The Roman ruins at Cerro da Vila, to the east of Albufeira, attest to this era and provide valuable insights into Roman domestic life, including fascinating bathhouses and mosaics.

After the fall of the Roman Empire, Albufeira, like many other areas of the Iberian Peninsula, was occupied by the Visigoths until the 8th century. Then came one of the most defining periods in Albufeira's history: the Moorish conquest. The Moors renamed the town "Al-

Buhera," meaning "Castle of the Sea." They fortified the town and constructed the impressive castle that would become a symbol of Albufeira. While the castle was destroyed in the 1755 earthquake, its impact lingers in the town's name.

The Christian Reconquista in 1249 brought Albufeira under Portuguese control. Over the centuries that followed, Albufeira transformed into a thriving fishing village. The town's economy was heavily reliant on fishing and farming, with a particular emphasis on almonds, figs, and carob.

Albufeira's Cultural Identity

The culture of Albufeira is a fascinating blend of its historical influences and modern day life. You can sense the Roman and Moorish influences in the ancient architecture of the Old Town, where narrow cobbled streets wind around white-washed buildings, leading to a central square, Largo Eng. Duarte Pacheco. This square, often filled with live music and vibrant stalls, embodies the spirit of Albufeira: a love for life, community, and celebration.

Portuguese traditions hold a strong presence in Albufeira's culture. This is vividly demonstrated in the town's numerous festivals. A notable celebration is the Festa do Pescador (Fisherman's Festival), held in September. It's a tribute to Albufeira's fishing heritage, featuring local cuisine, particularly seafood, folk music, and traditional dances.

Another prominent festival is the Festa de Nossa Senhora da Orada (Feast of Our Lady of Orada), a religious festival held in August. A maritime procession takes a statue of the patron saint from the Chapel of Nossa Senhora da Orada out to sea, asking for protection and a plentiful year of fishing.

The Influence of Tourism and Modernity

In the mid-20th century, Albufeira began its transformation into a popular tourist destination. The town quickly adapted to cater to an influx of international visitors, with restaurants, bars, and hotels springing up around the coastline and town center. This rise in tourism led to economic growth, but Albufeira has managed to maintain its unique cultural heritage while offering modern amenities and experiences to tourists.

The development of the Marina area is an example of this balance. The colorful buildings are a departure from the traditional architecture, but they add a distinct vibrancy to the town. The area is bustling with activity, offering boat tours, dolphin watching, diving, and fishing trips that not only entertain but also connect tourists with Albufeira's maritime roots.

Furthermore, the growth of tourism has allowed Albufeira to share its rich culinary culture with the world. Traditional Portuguese dishes, especially the region's seafood, have gained international acclaim. Dishes like Cataplana (a seafood stew), grilled sardines, and Piri-Piri chicken are served in many restaurants, inviting visitors to partake in Albufeira's gastronomic culture.

Local wines, particularly those from the Algarve region, have also gained prominence, and several places offer wine tasting experiences. It's not uncommon to see tourists enjoying a glass of Vinho Verde (a young Portuguese wine) while dining al fresco in the Old Town or along the beach, truly immersing themselves in the local lifestyle.

Albufeira Today: A Blend of Old and New

Today, Albufeira is a harmonious blend of the old and the new, the traditional and the modern. In the heart of the city, the Old Town bears testament to the past, with its charming cobblestone streets, traditional houses, and the remnants of the old castle wall. It's not hard to imagine the Albufeira of old, a quiet fishing town perched on the edge of the Atlantic.

Conversely, the newer parts of Albufeira, like the Strip in the Areias de São João area, represent the town's adaptation to tourism, boasting a multitude of bars, nightclubs, and shops. This area comes alive in the evening, offering a very different but equally essential part of the Albufeira experience.

Despite these developments, Albufeira has managed to retain its cultural authenticity. The city's history is proudly displayed, and traditional Portuguese lifestyles are celebrated. Albufeira has managed to open its doors to the world without losing its unique identity, which is perhaps why it remains such a beloved destination for so many.

From the echoes of the Romans and Moors in the Old Town streets to the lively energy of its modern tourist hotspots, the history and culture of Albufeira offer endless fascination. As you explore this captivating town, every corner reveals a new layer of its rich past and a new insight into its vibrant present, creating an unforgettable experience that truly encapsulates the essence of Albufeira.

2. Getting to Albufeira

Reaching Albufeira is relatively straightforward, given the range of transportation options available. Whether you prefer to travel by air, rail, or road, Albufeira is well-connected and easy to access from various parts of Portugal and beyond. While air travel remains the most time-efficient method, rail and bus services offer an affordable and enjoyable journey through Portugal's picturesque landscapes.

By train

If you're arriving from Oporto or Lisbon Airport, a train journey to Albufeira is a viable option. Several stations in these cities, as well as others across Portugal, provide direct trains or connections to Albufeira-Ferreiras station, located about 5 km north of the town center. The personnel at the train stations can guide you through the route, ensuring a smooth journey. As of 2023, a ticket from Lisbon to Albufeira costs around €20-30, and the journey takes approximately 3 hours.

For up-to-date timetables and to purchase tickets, visit the Comboios de Portugal (CP) website: https://www.cp.pt/passageiros/en/buy-tickets

For detailed station information, visit: https://www.cp.pt/passageiros/en/train-times/Stations/albufeira-ferreiras-station

By bus

An alternative way to reach Albufeira is by bus. Several bus terminals across Portugal offer services to Albufeira, providing flexibility in terms of departure points and times. Prices for bus tickets can range from €15 to €25 depending on the distance.

To purchase tickets and check the latest bus schedules, visit: https://www.rede-expressos.pt/en/tickets

For detailed station and route information, visit: http://eva-bus.com/estacoes_rodoviarias.php or https://www.rede-expressos.pt/en/

By Air

The Faro International Airport, also known as Algarve Airport, serves as the primary hub for tourists visiting Albufeira and the southern region of Portugal. The airport code for Faro is FAO. The airport is about a 40-minute drive from Albufeira and provides both international and domestic flights, with a focus on tourism and seasonal peaks. The majority of flights are from European countries such as the UK, Germany, the Netherlands, and the Republic of Ireland, representing over 80% of Faro's air traffic.

At present, Faro airport is served by various airlines, including the Portuguese airline TAP and the Irish low-cost carrier Ryanair. It offers direct flights from around 30 to 40 European cities, though the number can vary with the seasons. Booking flights early can help secure lower prices.

For detailed airport information, visit: https://www.aeroportodefaro.com/

Airlines that Fly to Faro

Here's a list of some airlines that offer connections to Faro:

- Aer Lingus, Air Berlin, Air Transat, British Airways
- EasyJet, Flybe, Iberia, Jet2, Lufthansa
- Monarch, Norwegian, Ryanair, Transavia
- TAP Portugal

Ensure to check with the individual airline for the most accurate and up-to-date flight schedules and prices.

From Faro Airport to Albufeira

We recommend considering a car rental for your journey from Faro Airport to Albufeira. With daily rates starting around €40, a rental car not only provides the convenience of setting your own schedule but also allows you to explore the area more freely. Given that public transportation in Albufeira is still in the development phase, having a personal vehicle can add a layer of comfort to your travel experience. However, there are also other viable options to consider.

BUS

Public bus service from Faro airport to Albufeira is primarily facilitated by the Circuit 16 Bus, commonly referred to as the "Pink Line." This service connects Faro city center with Faro beach (Ilha de Faro), passing through the airport in its route.

The bus stops at the airport are easily identifiable, situated under two large structures corresponding to the arrivals and departures sections. After exiting the arrivals area, simply follow the signs leading to the bus stop. It's conveniently located within a short walking distance, just in front of the terminal and adjacent to the taxi rank.

Regardless of your final destination in Albufeira, your initial journey will always be on the Circuit 16 bus, heading towards the terminal station at Faro city center. From there, you can connect to several bus routes to Albufeira, operated by the EVA Bus company.

For the latest timetable, ticket prices, and more information, click on this link: [**timetable and ticket price.**].

The map provided below indicates the exact locations of the two bus stops at the airport.

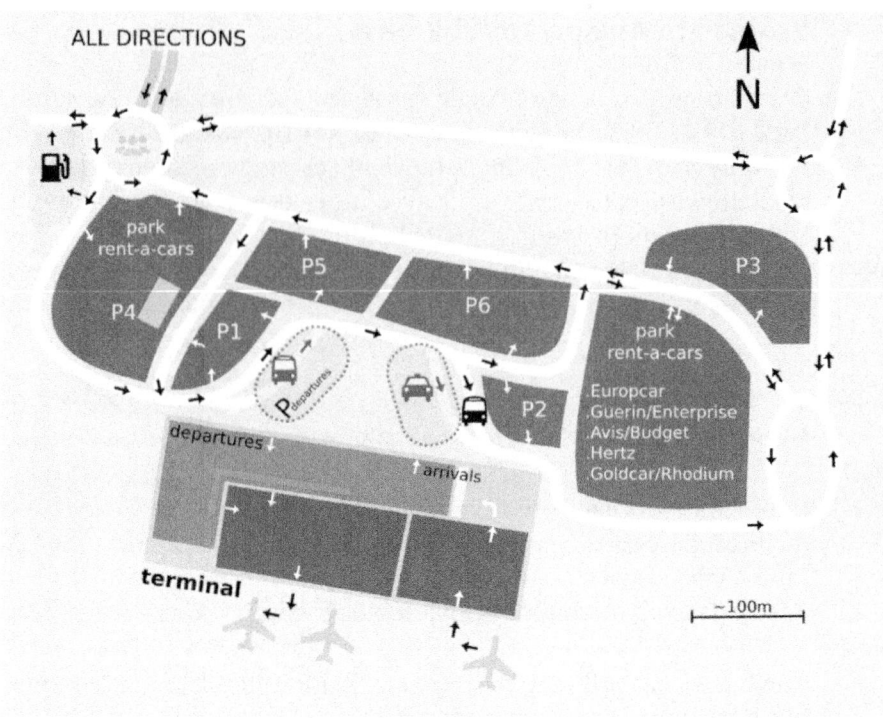

Image 2 - Bus 16 stops at the Faro Airport

For more information, click on this link:
https://en.aeroportodefaro.com/buses

TRAIN

Unfortunately, there is no direct rail link to Faro airport. However, the nearest train station in Faro city center is only 6 km away. There are several ways to complete your journey from Faro train station to Faro airport, including by taxi, bus, or private transfer.

By taxi

A taxi ride between Faro airport and the train station takes approximately 10 minutes under normal traffic conditions and costs about €11-€16. Taxis can be a convenient choice for individuals or small groups, particularly if you're traveling with heavy luggage.

By bus

If you're budget-conscious, consider taking the bus. Faro's central bus station is a mere 200-meter walk from the train station. To or from the airport, take the Circuit 16 bus. The journey takes about 20 minutes, with tickets priced at €2.25 per person.

By transfer

For a more personalized experience, you can arrange a private transfer between Faro airport and Faro train station. Taking approximately 10 minutes, the average price for a private transfer accommodating up to 4 passengers is €20, regardless of the time of day. Private transfers are particularly advantageous as they avoid wait times upon arrival and can be an economical choice for larger groups. You can book your transfer online in advance (transfers at Faro airport).

Once you arrive at Faro's train station, board the regional train heading to Lagos and disembark at Albufeira-Ferreiras station. This station is about 8 km from Albufeira's city center, and a one-way ticket costs €3.30.

From Albufeira-Ferreiras station, you can take the bus from the urban orange line for €1.40, which will take you to Albufeira's central bus terminal. Depending on your accommodation's location, a second bus journey may be necessary. Albufeira's urban bus routes are managed by the Giro company, and tickets are uniformly priced at €1.40.

Alternatively, you may prefer to take a taxi directly to your hotel once in Albufeira, available both at the train station and the bus terminal. This option can be quicker but will cost more than taking the bus.

More detailed information about the train service can be found at this link: https://en.aeroportodefaro.com/trains. Also have a look at Albufeira bus terminal, see bus lines map in Albufeira - the ticket price is 1,40€ for all lines.

GIRO

Giro is the urban bus in Albufeira. It has the Green, Blue, Orange, Red and Red 2 lines, and it makes connections between the city center, the marina, the camping site, Ferreiras (train station), Montechoro and Santa Eulália.

Click here to see bus lines map in Albufeira.

Tickets Price:
Normal ticket: 1,40 € (valid for 1 trip)
Tourist ticket: 4,00 €
(valid for one day, limitless trips on all the circuits)

Timetable:[1]
Monday to Sunday
October to May – 7:00am to 10:00pm
June to September – 7:00am to 10.00pm

SHUTTLE

A transfer between the airport and Albufeira will cost approximately 30€ per trip. You have to book it beforehand. To do that and see more details on this link: https://en.aeroportodefaro.com/transfers

TAXI

A taxi will cost around 40€ for a group of up to 4; and 52 € for a group of 4/7 people. Click on this link to know more or to book or call a taxi: http://taxipinheiro.com/transfers-from-faro-airport-to/albufeira

---

[1] *Tip:* Average waiting is of 30 minutes, except Saturdays starting at 2pm, Sundays and holidays during all day, in which the average waiting time is of one hour.

UBER

You can also choose the Uber service, which is now available in Algarve. The estimation for the distance between the airport and the Balaia Mar Hotel is between 32-43€.

Useful Telephone Numbers and Travel Information

Portugal's country code is +351 or 00351, so don't forget to type that if you want to make a call from or to a foreign mobile phone.

Telephone Numbers:

Lisbon Airport: +351 21 841 3500

Oporto Airport: +351 22 943 2400

Faro Airport: +351 289 800 800

Bus Station: +351 289 589 055

Train Station +351 707 210 220

Taxis: +351 289 583 230

Health Center: +351 289 598 400

Post Office: +351 289 580 860

Unicâmbio: +351 967819847

Emergencies/Police/Firemen: 112

Banks: Open from Monday to Friday 8-15pm.

ATM's: Spread throughout the whole city

Currency: Portugal's former official currency was the Escudo – PTE$. The current official currency, being part of the European Union, is the Euro – EUR€. The coins are issued in 1c, 2c, 5c, 10c, 20c, 50c, 1€ and 2€. All circulating coins have a common reverse, portraying a map of Europe, but each country in the Eurozone has its own design on the obverse, which means that each coin has a variety of different designs in circulation at once. Banknotes are issued in 5€, 10€, 20€, 50€, 100€, 200€, and 500€. Each banknote has its own color and is dedicated to an artistic period of European architecture. The front of the note features windows or gateways while the back has bridges, symbolizing links between countries and with the future.

Credit Cards: Most internationally recognized credit cards are accepted at restaurants and shops.

Time Zone: Portugal's time zone is WET (Western Europe Time) or UTC(Coordinated Universal Time) +0. During Summer, it is used in the WEST (Western Europe Summer Time) or DST (Daylight Saving Time), or UTC+1. The official format used is the 24hours format. So, every hour after 12 p.m. would just go on until the 24th hour, instead of just going back to 1 p.m. This way, the official way to say the time if it is 4 p.m. would be 16h since 1 p.m. – 13h; 2 p.m. – 14h; 3 p.m. – 15h. In spite of this, in informal conversations, it is more common to use «*da manhã*» or «*da tarde/da noite*.»

3. Getting Around Albufeira

Albufeira, despite being a popular tourist destination, is a relatively compact city. This makes getting around quite straightforward, whether by public transportation, rented vehicles, or on foot. Here's a comprehensive guide to your options:

3.1 Public Transportation

Giro Buses: Giro is the local bus service, with Green, Blue, Orange, Red, and Red 2 lines connecting various parts of the city. The routes cover the city center, marina, campsite, Ferreiras train station, Montechoro, and Santa Eulália. Tickets cost €1.40 per ride, or €4.00 for a day pass with unlimited trips. More information about routes, schedules, and tickets can be found at [insert website link here].

Regional Trains: For journeys beyond Albufeira, regional trains are a comfortable and cost-effective option. The Albufeira-Ferreiras train station, approximately 8 km from the city center, connects Albufeira to other towns in the Algarve and across Portugal. Information about train times and fares can be found at https://www.cp.pt/passageiros/en.

3.2 Car Rentals

Renting a car provides the most flexibility when exploring Albufeira and the surrounding areas.

There are several car rental agencies in Albufeira, including international brands like Hertz, Avis, and Budget, as well as local companies. A standard economy car usually starts around €40 per day, although prices can fluctuate based on the season and availability. Always remember to book in advance, especially during the peak tourist season. Car rental companies typically require drivers to be at least 21 years old, and additional charges may apply for drivers under 25.

3.3 Bikes and Scooters

Renting a bike or scooter can be an enjoyable and eco-friendly way to explore Albufeira.

Bikes: There are several places to rent bikes in Albufeira. Prices start around €15 per day for a standard bike, with discounts often available for longer rentals. Companies like Albufeira Bike Rental (http://www.albufeirabikerental.com) offer a range of options, from city bikes to mountain bikes.

Scooters: Scooter rentals are also popular, with prices starting around €30 per day. These can be an efficient way to navigate Albufeira's streets, especially during busier periods. Helmets are usually included in the rental price, and remember that you'll need a valid driving license to rent a scooter.

3.4 Walking

Given Albufeira's relatively compact size, walking is often the easiest way to get around, especially within the city center.

The city is very pedestrian-friendly, with numerous well-signposted walking routes. Walking allows you to truly experience Albufeira's charm, from its cobbled streets and bustling markets to the stunning coastline. Always ensure you have a good map or smartphone with GPS capabilities to help navigate the city's winding streets.

Remember, however, that Albufeira is quite hilly in places, so comfortable walking shoes are a must. And always carry water, especially in the summer months when temperatures can soar.

4. Accommodation

4.1 Best Areas to Stay in Albufeira

Choosing where to stay in Albufeira depends largely on what you want out of your visit. Here's a breakdown of some of the best areas to stay in, depending on your preferences:

1. Old Town

The Old Town is the historic heart of Albufeira, characterized by narrow, winding cobblestone streets, vibrant squares, and a plethora of bars, restaurants, and shops. Staying here, you're within walking distance of a beautiful sandy beach, Pescadores Beach, and the lively main square that hosts entertainment and music performances throughout the year.

Recommended for: Visitors looking for a blend of history, culture, and nightlife.

2. Praia da Oura and Areias de São João (The Strip)

Praia da Oura is a modern, lively area known for 'The Strip', a street packed with bars, restaurants, and nightclubs. It's perfect for those seeking a vibrant nightlife scene. Oura Beach is a beautiful spot for sunbathing and watersports, and the area has a wide variety of accommodations to suit all budgets.

Recommended for: Younger travelers or those looking for nightlife.

3. Albufeira Marina

The Marina area of Albufeira, painted in pastel colors, is a fantastic choice for families or those seeking a quieter, more relaxed stay. Here you'll find plenty of restaurants and cafes with stunning views, boat tours, and family-friendly activities such as the Hot Wheels Raceway indoor karting track. It's a short walk from the Old Town and its beaches.

Recommended for: Families and visitors seeking a quieter holiday.

4. São Rafael

São Rafael is a tranquil, upscale area known for its stunning natural beauty. It's home to some of the best beaches in Albufeira, such as Praia de São Rafael and Praia do Castelo. Here you'll find luxury resorts and villas nestled amidst scenic landscapes. It's a great base for exploring the natural beauty of the Algarve.

Recommended for: Visitors seeking a quiet, luxurious, and scenic beachside holiday.

5. Gale (Praia Gale)

Located west of Albufeira, Gale is a peaceful residential area known for its long stretch of sandy beach, Praia da Gale. The area offers a mix of high-end villas, self-catering apartments, and hotels. It's an excellent location for those who prefer a slower pace, but still want to be within easy reach of the main attractions.

Recommended for: Those looking for a relaxed, beach-centric vacation.

Remember, no matter where you choose to stay, Albufeira is relatively compact, and it's easy to get from one part of the city to another. So, even if you opt for the tranquillity of Gale or São Rafael, the bustling nightlife of The Strip or the charming history of the Old Town are just a short trip away.

6. Montechoro

Montechoro is an area of Albufeira that is popular with families and couples alike, thanks to its great location and wide range of amenities. It's a peaceful suburb that's just a stone's throw away from the buzz of the Strip, and a short distance from beautiful beaches like Praia da Oura. The Montechoro Strip is lined with a range of international restaurants, bars, and shops, so you'll have everything you need close by.

Recommended for: Families and couples looking for a peaceful base with amenities at their fingertips.

7. Olhos de Água

A charming former fishing village, Olhos de Água is ideal for those looking for a more traditional and tranquil Algarve experience. It still retains much of its original character, with local fishermen hauling in their catch on the beach. The area boasts beautiful beaches, like Praia de Belharucas and Praia de Maria Luísa, and is surrounded by countryside for walking and cycling.

Recommended for: Those wanting a taste of traditional Algarve.

8. Albufeira City Center

If you want to be at the heart of the action, consider staying in Albufeira City Center. This area has a bit of everything - beautiful beaches, a vibrant nightlife, abundant shopping opportunities, and a broad range of eateries. It's also home to several popular tourist attractions and offers easy access to transportation options for exploring further afield.

Recommended for: Visitors wanting to be in the middle of the action, with everything on their doorstep.

9. Balaia

Situated between Albufeira and Olhos de Água, Balaia is a calm residential area with several high-quality resorts. This area is home to some fantastic beaches and coves, and is also renowned for the Balaia Golf Course. It's a great option if you're looking for a resort-style holiday with all the amenities.

Recommended for: Golf enthusiasts and those seeking a resort-style stay.

Remember, wherever you choose to stay in Albufeira, it's easy to explore other parts of this beautiful city due to the excellent public transportation links and affordable taxi services.

4.1 Luxury Hotels

Vila Joya

Nestled right next to the pristine Galé Beach, the exquisite Vila Joya offers an unforgettable luxury experience. With its soft white sand and sparkling turquoise waters, the beach is a perfect backdrop for this exquisite property. However, Vila Joya's crowning glory is its world-renowned restaurant, which has been awarded two Michelin stars. Here, guests can savor gourmet cuisine that perfectly blends traditional Portuguese ingredients with innovative culinary techniques. The accommodation itself echoes the high standards of its restaurant, with meticulously designed rooms that encapsulate luxury and comfort.

For those interested in experiencing Vila Joya's culinary delights, book a table via the following link: Vila Joya - Restaurant Booking.

If you wish to stay in this sumptuous villa, view more details and book rooms online via this link: Vila Joya.

Address: Estrada da Galé, 8201-917 Albufeira **Tel**: +351 289 591 795
E-mail: info@vilajoya.com

Price per night: Rates start from 545€ per night

Image 4 - One of the signatures dishes of the Vila Joya Restaurant

Salgados Dunas Suites

Experience luxury amid nature at Salgados Dunas Suites. This opulent hotel is situated a stone's throw away from the endless Salgados beach and is set within a preserved natural area. Its rooms offer stunning views of the ocean and the picturesque natural sand dunes. Whether you prefer lounging by one of their seven outdoor pools or exploring the natural beauty of the area, Salgados Dunas Suites ensures an unforgettable stay.

For more details and to book rooms online, click on this link: Salgados Dunas Suites

Address: Herdade dos Salgados Resort, Rua Boca da Alagoa, 8200-424 Albufeira **Tel**: +351 289 244 780 **E-mail**: salgadosdunas@nauhotels.com **Price per night**: Rates start from 115€ per night

Pine Cliffs Resort

Perched atop striking red cliffs overlooking the Atlantic Ocean, Pine Cliffs Resort is another gem for those seeking an unparalleled luxury experience. This award-winning resort features stunning rooms, suites, and villas, a 9-hole golf course, Serenity - The Art of Well Being spa, and a plethora of dining options. With a rich array of amenities and activities, Pine Cliffs caters to all ages and interests.

Discover more and book your stay through the following link: Pine Cliffs Resort

Address: Praia Da Falésia, PO Box 644, Albufeira **Tel**: +351 289 500 100 **E-mail**: info@pinecliffs.com **Price per night**: Rates available upon request

4.2 Mid-range Hotels

Boavista

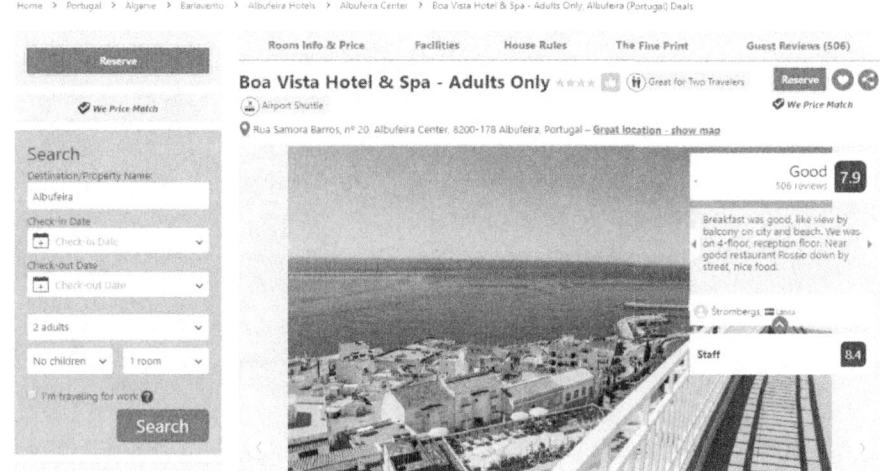

Hotel Boavista is a charming hotel that offers breathtaking views from its rooms and balconies. Its convenient location near the city center makes it a perfect choice for those seeking the lively hustle of Albufeira without compromising the tranquility of their accommodation. The hotel's restaurant is an established name for its scrumptious traditional regional dishes, making it a favored dining spot for both guests and locals alike.

For booking your stay online, use this link: Hotel Boavista Booking. For more detailed information about the hotel, click here: Hotel Boavista Info.

Address: Rua Samora Barros 20. 8200-178 Albufeira **Tel**: +351 289 589 175 **E-mail**: hotelboavista@hoteis-belver.pt **Price per night**: Rates start from 95€ per night

Real Bellavista Hotel & Spa

Situated near the football stadium, Real Bellavista Hotel & Spa is a hotel that seamlessly blends quality services with value for money. This hotel is committed to ensuring a relaxing and comfortable holiday for its guests, providing a wide range of services including wellness treatments at their on-site spa, various dining options, and a dedicated concierge service.

Book your stay and find more information online using this link: Hotel Real Bellavista Booking and Info.

Address: Rua do Estádio, 8200-127 Albufeira **Tel**: +351 289 540 060 **E-mail**: reservas.alg@hoteisreal.com or info@realbellavista.com **Price per night**: Rates start from 63€ per night

Hotel Sol e Mar

Located directly on the beach in the heart of Albufeira, Hotel Sol e Mar offers stunning views of the Atlantic Ocean. Each room features a private balcony where guests can enjoy the spectacular views. This hotel is particularly favored for its proximity to Albufeira's Old Town and its vibrant array of shops, bars, and restaurants.

Find more details and book rooms online through this link: Hotel Sol e Mar

Address: Rua Bernardino de Sousa, 8200-146 Albufeira **Tel**: +351 289 580 500 **E-mail**: geral@hotelsolalbufeira.com **Price per night**: Rates available upon request

4.3 Budget Options

Hotel da Aldeia

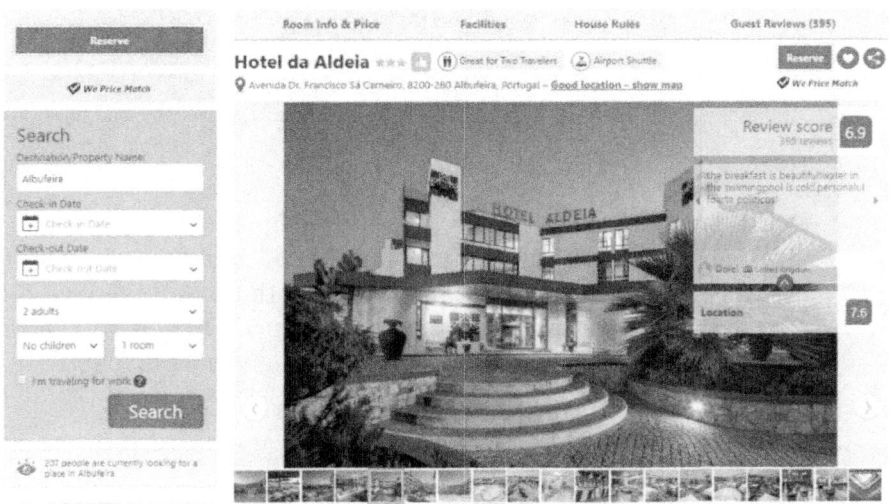

Situated right on The Strip, Hotel da Aldeia is an excellent choice for those looking to indulge in Albufeira's vibrant nightlife scene. Its prime location ensures you're only steps away from the action, yet it provides a peaceful retreat to recharge when the party winds down.

To make a booking online, follow this link: Hotel da Aldeia Booking. For further information about the hotel, click on this link: Hotel da Aldeia Info.

Address: Areias de São João 280, 8200-270 Albufeira **Tel**: +351 289 588 861 **E-mail**: hotelaldeia@hoteis-belver.pt

Price per night: Rates start from 54€ per night

Inatel

Positioned atop the Inatel Beach and conveniently located just a short six-minute stroll from the city center, Inatel Hotel is a popular budget-friendly option for travelers. Its prime location, combined with its comfortable accommodation, make it a desirable choice for those seeking affordability without compromising on comfort and accessibility.

To book your stay or find more information, click on this link: Hotel do Inatel Booking and Info.

Address: Av. Infante D. Henrique, 8200-862 Albufeira **Tel**: +351 289 599 300 **E-mail**: inatel.albufeira@inatel.pt **Price per night**: Rates start from 48€ per night

Price per night: Available from 48€

Hotel Frentomar

For travelers seeking an affordable option in Albufeira, Hotel Frentomar is a perfect choice. It offers a great location close to the beach, clean rooms, and friendly service. This budget hotel ensures you can enjoy your stay in Albufeira without breaking the bank.

For more information and to book your stay, visit this link: Hotel Frentomar Booking.

Address: Rua General Humberto Delgado 7, 8200-268 Albufeira **Tel**: +351 289 589 102 **E-mail**: info@frentomar.com **Price per night**: Rates available upon request

4.4 ApartHotels

Alfagar Aparthotel

You are just an 8-minute walk away from the Santa Eulália beach. Highly reviewed by many customers, this aparthotel has a fully equipped kitchenette.

For booking online, click on this link: Alfagar Aparthotel Booking. For more information about the aparthotel, click here: Alfagar Aparthotel Info

Address: Santa Eulália-Balaia, 8200-912 Albufeira, **Tel.:** +351 289 540 220, **E-mail**: reservas@alfagar.com

Price per night: Available from 62€

Golden Beach by 3HB

With a fully equipped kitchenette, this aparthotel is just 2 minutes away, on foot, from the Oura beach. Several restaurants, bars, and nightclubs are within 280 m.

For booking online, click on this link: Golden Beach by 3HB Booking. For more info, click on this link: Golden Beach by 3HB info

Address: Rua Ramalho Ortigão - Praia Da Oura, 8200-604 Albufeira, Portugal, **Tel.:** +351 289 586 160, **E-mail:** info@3hb.com

Price per night: Available from 95€

4.5 Our Top Hotel Suggestion

Our favorite hotel recommendation for Albufeira is the Balaia Mar Hotel.

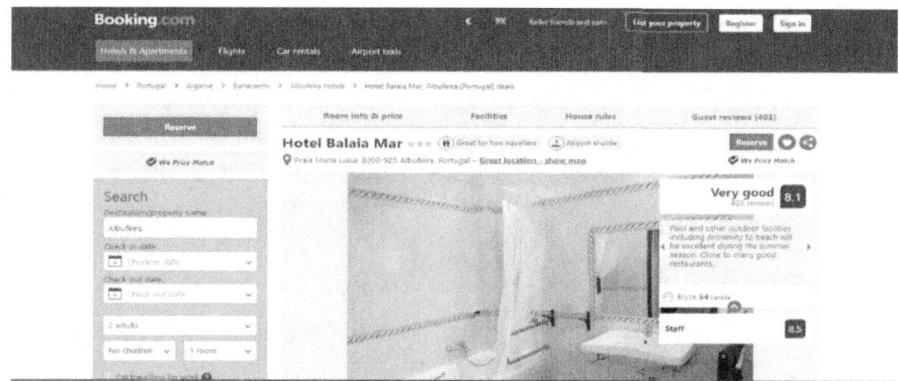

It is the hotel that offers the best value for money. However, other options were given precisely to fit and cater to whatever your needs may be. So, feel free to choose from those suggestions. Know that you can also follow the same three days' itinerary plan if you decide to stay at any other hotel in Albufeira. Guidora does not have any affiliation with any of these hotels.

Image 3 - Balaia Mar Hotel - Swimming Pool

Address: Praia Maria Luísa, 8200-925 Albufeira

Tel.: +351 289 590 800

E-mail: reservas@balaia.com

Price per night: Available from 100€

5. Sightseeing in Albufeira

5.1 Historical Landmarks

Castle of Paderne

[handwritten: No 10km from Town]

The Castle of Paderne, located just a few kilometers from the center of Albufeira, is one of the seven castles featured on the Portuguese flag. Built in the 12th century by the Moors, it's now in ruins but still offers a glimpse into the country's rich history. Its setting near the Quarteira river, along with its wildflowers and wildlife, makes it a wonderful place for a leisurely walk. There's no entrance fee, and it's accessible throughout the year.

For more details, visit Castle of Paderne.

Church of São Sebastião (Igreja Matriz de Albufeira)

Located in Albufeira's old town, the Church of São Sebastião is a 18th-century building known for its stunning architecture and beautiful Manueline doorway. Inside, you can admire the gilded woodwork and the beautiful tile panels depicting scenes from the life of Saint Sebastian.

The church is usually open every day from 9.30am to 12.30pm and then again from 3pm to 5pm. Entrance is free, but donations are welcome.

For more information, visit Church of São Sebastião.

Museum of Sacred Art (Museu de Arte Sacra)

Situated inside the Chapel of San Sebastian, the Museum of Sacred Art houses a rich collection of religious art dating back to the 16th century. Highlights include a Gothic style monstrance, a silver processional cross from the 16th century, and many more religious artifacts.

The museum is open from Monday to Friday, 9.30am to 12.30pm and 2pm to 5pm. Admission fee is 1€.

For more details, visit Museum of Sacred Art.

Torre do Relógio (Clock Tower)

The Clock Tower is one of the city's main historical symbols. Built in the 19th century on top of one of the former castle towers, it is easily recognizable for its wrought iron bell structure. The tower isn't usually open to the public, but its beauty can be appreciated from many points in the old town.

For more details, visit Clock Tower.

Roman Ruins of Cerro da Vila

Located in nearby Vilamoura, the Roman Ruins of Cerro da Vila house the remains of a Roman villa dating back to the 1st century. Here, you can explore ancient baths, residential foundations, and beautifully preserved mosaics. There's also a museum on-site.

The site is open from Tuesday to Sunday, from 9.30am to 12.30pm and from 2pm to 6pm. The entrance fee is 3€.

For more information, visit Roman Ruins of Cerro da Vila.

Municipal Museum of Archaeology of Albufeira (Museu Municipal de Arqueologia)

Located in the old town of Albufeira, the Municipal Museum of Archaeology provides visitors with a comprehensive look at the city's rich history, from prehistoric times to the present day. The museum's collection includes prehistoric artifacts, Roman pottery, Moorish oil lamps, and various exhibits from the 15th to the 17th centuries.

The museum is open from Tuesday to Sunday, from 9.30am to 5.30pm. The entrance fee is 2€.

For more information, visit Municipal Museum of Archaeology.

Chapel of Our Lady of Orada (Ermida de Nossa Senhora da Orada)

This humble yet charming chapel located in the Marina of Albufeira holds significant religious importance in the city. The chapel is a pilgrimage site for many during the annual Feast of Our Lady of Orada, held on August 15th.

The chapel is usually open in the mornings and for Sunday Mass. There's no admission fee, but it's advisable to check the opening hours ahead of your visit.

For more information, visit Chapel of Our Lady of Orada.

Old Town of Albufeira

Though not a specific landmark, Albufeira's Old Town is a historical treasure in itself. With its cobbled streets, traditional Portuguese buildings, vibrant squares, and an abundance of shops, bars, and restaurants, it is the heart and soul of the city. Explore the area on foot to soak in its lively atmosphere and historical charm.

For more details, visit Old Town Albufeira.

Remember to always check the official websites or local tourist information centers for the most up-to-date information, as opening hours and admission fees may vary.

5.2 Beaches

Albufeira is home to some of the most beautiful and scenic beaches in Portugal. Its coast, blessed with golden sands, turquoise waters, and dramatic cliffs, offers a beach experience like no other.

Praia dos Pescadores (Fishermen's Beach)

One of the most famous beaches in Albufeira, Praia dos Pescadores, is located right next to the old town. It's a hub of activity with numerous restaurants and bars lining the promenade. The beach offers plenty of water sports and boat trips. There is no entrance fee and it's accessible year-round, though it can get crowded in the high season.

For more information, visit Praia dos Pescadores.

Praia da Oura (Oura Beach)

Nestled between Albufeira's bustling nightlife and the quieter old town, Oura Beach offers a balance of relaxation and entertainment. The golden sands and clear waters make for great swimming and sunbathing. Beach bars and restaurants are just a stone's throw away.

For more details, visit Praia da Oura.

Praia de São Rafael (São Rafael Beach)

This is a tranquil and picturesque beach known for its striking rock formations, crystal clear water, and lush vegetation. It's an ideal spot for snorkeling due to its abundant marine life. São Rafael is a bit quieter compared to the city center beaches, offering a more relaxed experience.

For more information, visit Praia de São Rafael.

Praia da Galé (Galé Beach)

Galé Beach is known for its long stretch of sand and calm, shallow waters, making it a perfect family-friendly beach. To the west of the beach, you can enjoy a more secluded and natural setting with fascinating rock formations.

For more details, visit Praia da Galé.

Praia dos Salgados (Salgados Beach)

This extensive beach offers plenty of space for beachgoers and is often less crowded. It's located next to the Salgados Lagoon, a haven for bird watchers with many species visiting throughout the year.

For more information, visit Praia dos Salgados.

5.3 Nature and Parks

Parque Natural da Ria Formosa

This expansive nature park spans over 18,000 hectares and includes a variety of habitats from marshes to sand dunes. It's an ideal place for bird watching, with over 200 species recorded here. Boat tours are available for exploring the various islets and lagoons.

For more details, visit Parque Natural da Ria Formosa.

Zoomarine Algarve

An amazing theme park combining fun rides, exhibitions, and animal shows. It's particularly renowned for its dolphin show. There's also a chance to relax at the man-made beach and swimming areas. It's a great day out for the whole family.

For tickets and opening hours, visit Zoomarine Algarve.

5.4 Museums and Galleries

Museu Municipal de Arqueologia de Albufeira

This local museum showcases Albufeira's rich history through its archaeology, from the prehistoric times to the present. The museum is located in Albufeira's old town.

For more details, visit Museu Municipal de Arqueologia de Albufeira.

Galeria de Arte Pintor Samora Barros

This art gallery features the works of the famous Portuguese artist Samora Barros and other local and international artists. It's located in the heart of Albufeira's old town.

For more information, visit Galeria de Arte Pintor Samora Barros.

Sacred Art Museum of Albufeira

A small museum housing religious artifacts and showcasing the town's Christian heritage, the Sacred Art Museum is situated within the Chapel of St. Sebastian (Capela de São Sebastião). It features various statues, paintings, and pieces of sacred art dating back to the 18th century.

Address: Rua da Igreja Nova, 8200 Albufeira. No online presence found as of my knowledge cutoff in September 2021.

5.5 Religious Sites

Igreja de Sant'Ana

This charming church dates back to the 18th century and features a beautiful combination of Baroque and Neoclassical architectural styles. It's a peaceful spot in the heart of Albufeira's old town.

For more details, visit Igreja de Sant'Ana.

Igreja Matriz

Also known as the Mother Church, Igreja Matriz is one of the most significant religious landmarks in Albufeira. Built in the late 18th century, the church showcases a unique blend of Neoclassical and Baroque styles.

For more information, visit Igreja Matriz.

Igreja de São Sebastião

Located in the heart of Albufeira, Igreja de São Sebastião is a notable example of 18th-century Portuguese architecture. With its beautiful tiles (azulejos) and impressive bell tower, it is a significant spiritual and cultural landmark in the town.

Address: Rua da Igreja Nova, 8200 Albufeira. There's no entry fee for the church, and it's generally open during daylight hours.

6. Activities and Experiences

6.1 Water Sports

Water sports are a major attraction in Albufeira, with its stunning beaches and crystal-clear waters providing an ideal playground. Here are a few water sports operators in Albufeira.

Albufeira Watersports Centre

Offers a wide range of thrilling water sports activities including jet skiing, parasailing, and banana boat rides. They also organize dolphin watching tours and fishing excursions.

Website: [Albufeira Watersports Centre](#) Address: Marina de Albufeira, 8200-394 Albufeira, Tel: +351 289 301 884.

Dolphins Driven

Provides unforgettable experiences of sea cave tours, dolphin watching, and private boat tours. They are known for their eco-conscious approach towards marine tourism.

Website: [Dolphins Driven](#) Address: Marina de Albufeira, 8200-394 Albufeira, Tel: +351 926 942 066.

Dream Wave Algarve

Offers a variety of water sports activities, including jet ski rentals, wakeboarding, and water skiing. They also provide boat tours to explore Albufeira's coastline and caves.

Website: [Dream Wave Algarve](#) Address: Marina de Albufeira, 8200-394 Albufeira, Tel: +351 962 003 885.

6.2 Golf Courses

The Algarve region is a paradise for golf lovers, boasting some of the finest golf courses in Europe. Here are a few notable golf courses in and around Albufeira.

- **Salgados Golf Course**

A beautiful 18-hole course set in a nature reserve with stunning ocean views. The layout is characterized by large greens and water hazards, providing a challenge for all skill levels.

Website: Salgados Golf Course Address: Herdade dos Salgados, R. Boca da Alagoa, 8200-424 Guia, Albufeira, Tel: +351 289 583 030.

- **Pine Cliffs Golf Course**

This 9-hole course offers stunning cliff-top views over the Atlantic. The "Devil's Parlour," a challenging par-3 across a ravine, is a highlight.

Website: Pine Cliffs Golf Course Address: Pinhal do Concelho, Praia da Falesia, 8200-912 Albufeira, Tel: +351 289 500 100.

- **Balaia Golf Village**

Featuring a 9-hole par-3 course, it's a great place for beginners or for those wishing to improve their short game. They also have a golf academy offering coaching for all ages and skill levels.

Website: Balaia Golf Village Address: Balaia Golf Village, 8200-594 Albufeira, Tel: +351 289 570 442.

Remember to check with each service provider for their current operating status and health and safety protocols. Prices can vary greatly depending on the season, time of day, and specific service or package you choose, so it's recommended to contact the providers directly or visit their websites for the most accurate and up-to-date information

6.3 Hiking and Cycling Trails

Albufeira's natural landscapes offer some excellent opportunities for hiking and cycling. Here are some of the best trails in the area:

The Seven Hanging Valleys Trail

This is one of the most beautiful hiking trails in the Algarve, offering breathtaking views of the coastline and the sea. The 11.4 km trail takes you along the clifftops between the Praia da Marinha beach and the Praia de Vale Centeanes.

Website for trail information: Seven Hanging Valleys Trail

Via Algarviana

This long-distance cycling and hiking trail spans the entire length of the Algarve from Alcoutim in the east to Cabo de São Vicente in the west. There are various entry and exit points along the way if you wish to tackle smaller sections.

Website for trail information: Via Algarviana

Ecovia do Litoral

This cycling route connects Cape St. Vincent to Vila Real de Santo António following the Algarve coast. It passes through Albufeira, allowing you to enjoy its stunning coastal scenery.

Website for trail information: Ecovia do Litoral

6.4 Nightlife

Albufeira is known for its vibrant nightlife, with a wealth of bars, clubs, and venues offering entertainment into the early hours. Here are some standout spots:

- **The Strip**

This is the heart of Albufeira's nightlife, a street packed with bars, clubs, and restaurants. Whether you want to enjoy live music, watch sports, or dance the night away, there's something for everyone here.

- **Old Town Albufeira**

For a more laid-back evening, head to the Old Town. Here, you'll find charming cobblestone streets lined with a variety of bars and restaurants. The main square is a hub of evening entertainment, with live music and street performers adding to the atmosphere.

- **Club Vida**

As one of Albufeira's top clubs, Club Vida offers a spacious dance floor, top DJs, and a stylish lounge area. It's the place to be for dance music lovers.

Address: Avenida Dr. Francisco Sá Carneiro, 8200-262 Albufeira, Tel: +351 912 577 374.

- **Kiss Disco Club**

This legendary club is known for its themed parties and hosts some of the biggest DJ names in Portugal. It's a must-visit for anyone looking for an unforgettable night out.

Address: Avenida Sá Carneiro, Areias de São João, 8200-340 Albufeira, Tel: +351 963 491 605.

6.5 Family Friendly Activities

There is a wealth of activities in Albufeira that families can enjoy together:

Zoomarine Algarve: This is more than just an aquarium. It's a place where you can see presentations with dolphins, seals, and sea lions, along with tropical birds and birds of prey. There's also a fantastic 4D cinema, and an amusement park with a ferris wheel, carousels, and more. To top it all off, the park has a beach area with a wave pool and waterslides, perfect for cooling off.

Website: Zoomarine Algarve Address: N125 KM 65, Guia, 8201-864 Albufeira, Tel.: +351 289 560 300, E-mail: info@zoomarine.pt Tickets: Available from 29€ for adults and 21€ for children (ages 4-10)

Aqualand Algarve: One of Portugal's largest water parks, Aqualand Algarve is packed with thrilling slides, a wave pool, and a children's paradise area for younger kids.

Website: Aqualand Algarve Address: E.N. 125 Sítio das Areias, 8365-908 Alcantarilha, Tel.: +351 282 320 230, E-mail: info@aqualand.pt Tickets: Available from 26€ for adults and 19€ for children (ages 5-10)

6.6 Spa and Wellness Centers

For those seeking relaxation and rejuvenation, Albufeira offers a variety of wellness centers and spas:

Serenity - The Art of Well Being: Located in the Pine Cliffs Resort, Serenity offers a comprehensive range of wellness services, from massages and facials to body treatments and wellness programs.

Website: Serenity Spa Address: Pine Cliffs Resort, Praia da Falésia, 8200-909 Albufeira, Tel.: +351 289 500 100, E-mail: serenity.algarve@luxurycollection.com

Almond Tree Wellness Spa: This wellness center, located at the Albufeira Resort, offers a variety of services including body treatments, massages, and wellness packages. They also offer specialized treatments like reflexology and hot stone massages.

Website: Almond Tree Wellness Spa Address: Vale de Carro, Albufeira, 8200-918 Albufeira, Tel.: +351 289 007 400, E-mail: spa@algarveresort.com

Remember to book your appointments in advance to secure your preferred dates and times.

7. Dining and Cuisine

7.1 Portuguese Cuisine

Portugal boasts an exceptionally diverse and delectable culinary scene. The food is bountiful and packed with unique flavours that are sure to tantalize your taste buds! There are numerous must-try dishes during your visit. Naturally, it would be challenging (and perhaps stomach-stretching) to sample everything in one visit; hence, we've curated a selection for you to seek out during your time in Albufeira or Portugal, or even to look for back in your local supermarket once you're home.

Açorda

Acorda is a quintessential dish from the southern regions of Portugal, including the Algarve. This hearty bread soup is a delightful example of Portuguese cuisine's ability to transform simple, rustic ingredients into a comforting and flavorful dish.

The basic ingredients of Acorda are stale bread, garlic, coriander, olive oil, vinegar, water, salt, and eggs. Depending on the version, it may also include seafood such as shrimp or cod, or meat like pork. The bread soaks up the savory broth and the dish is usually topped with a poached egg, making for a deliciously warming and satisfying meal.

Despite its humble origins as peasant food, Acorda has been embraced by chefs nationwide and can be found in many upscale restaurants, where it's often given a gourmet twist.

Whether enjoyed as a starter, main dish, or late-night comfort food, Acorda embodies the essence of Portuguese cuisine: simple, hearty, and full of flavor.

Xarém

Xarém is another iconic dish from the Algarve region, characterized by its comforting and homely nature. This rich cornmeal porridge, also known as polenta in other parts of the world, is deeply ingrained in the culinary heritage of southern Portugal.

The primary ingredient in Xarém is cornmeal, which is slowly cooked until it reaches a creamy consistency. The dish is then enhanced with a variety of accompaniments, depending on regional traditions and personal preferences. It could range from shellfish, meat, or a mix of both.

Popular variations of Xarém include additions like clams (Xarém com Conquilhas) or cuttlefish (Xarém com Chocos), providing a delightful contrast in texture and flavor. Other versions incorporate pork, making the dish even more hearty.

In many ways, Xarém is representative of the Algarve's culinary philosophy: simple, hearty dishes that make the most out of locally available ingredients. This classic dish is a must-try for anyone seeking an authentic taste of Portuguese cuisine. Be it at a traditional tasca or a modern restaurant, Xarém is a satisfying experience that will make your culinary journey in Albufeira even more memorable.

Cataplana

Cataplana is not just a staple dish of Algarve cuisine; it's also the name of the unique, clam-shaped copper cookware in which it's traditionally prepared. The dish embodies the region's love for seafood, featuring a flavorful blend of fish, shellfish, and local ingredients.

The typical Cataplana recipe includes a mix of seafood like clams, shrimp, and white fish, combined with chorizo, bell peppers, tomatoes, onions, garlic, and a dash of white wine. All these ingredients are cooked together in the sealed cataplana, which allows the flavors to meld together and intensify as the dish steams.

One of the highlights of eating Cataplana is the moment the cookware is opened at the table, releasing an enticing aroma of the sea mingled with the savory elements of the dish. This mouth-watering delight truly encapsulates the essence of Algarve's abundant coastline.

Remember, the best Cataplana is made with the freshest seafood, so be sure to indulge in this dish while dining near the beach or at a reputable seafood restaurant. Every bite offers a taste of the Algarve's rich culinary heritage and the bounty of its waters. If you're a seafood lover, Cataplana is an absolute must-try when visiting Albufeira.

Sardinhas

In Portugal, and especially in the coastal towns such as Albufeira, sardinhas (sardines) are a beloved staple and a highlight of summer cuisine. The Portuguese passion for sardines is well-known, with the peak season running from June to September. During this time, you'll often catch the enticing scent of sardines grilling in the open air, a telltale sign that summer has truly arrived.

Simplicity is key when preparing sardinhas. Typically, the fresh sardines are simply seasoned with coarse sea salt before being grilled over hot charcoal. The result is a wonderfully smoky, crisp skin that contrasts perfectly with the moist, flavorful flesh within.

Grilled sardines are traditionally served on a slice of bread which soaks up the fish's delicious juices. Accompanied by a simple salad of tomatoes, peppers, and onions dressed with olive oil and vinegar, this dish is a perfect example of the straightforward, yet flavorful, Mediterranean diet.

Every year, there are sardine festivals (sardinhas festas) throughout Portugal, where locals and tourists alike come together to enjoy this iconic dish. In Albufeira, dining on grilled sardines with a view of the sea is an experience not to be missed. Be sure to pair it with a glass of crisp vinho verde (young green wine) for an authentic Portuguese meal.

Whether you're a seafood enthusiast or a casual foodie, trying sardinhas in Albufeira is a must. It truly is a quintessential Portuguese experience!

Dom Rodrigo

Dom Rodrigo is a traditional Portuguese dessert native to the Algarve region, and it's a must-try for any sweet tooth visiting Albufeira. The name of the dessert, which translates to "King Rodrigo," is steeped in history and reflects the region's Moorish heritage.

Each Dom Rodrigo is a small, round sweet made from egg yolks, sugar, and ground almonds, all carefully wrapped in a foil package that makes it look like a precious gift. Its distinct shape and packaging are inspired by the Moorish tradition of wrapping sweets in bright, colorful foil.

Inside, the dessert is a delightful mix of textures. The egg yolk and sugar create a creamy, rich custard, while the ground almonds provide a slight crunch. Sometimes, the mixture is flavored with a hint of orange blossom water or lemon zest, adding a subtle citrusy note to the dessert.

Dom Rodrigos are typically served chilled, making them a refreshing treat on a hot Algarve day. They are often enjoyed with a strong espresso or a glass of medronho, a potent local fruit brandy, which balance the dessert's sweetness with their strong, bold flavors.

Available in local bakeries, cafes, and even at roadside stands, Dom Rodrigo is an Algarve culinary highlight. Whether enjoyed as a quick snack or as a dessert after a hearty meal, this delicacy encapsulates the rich flavors and history of the Algarve.

Remember that each Dom Rodrigo is quite rich, so you might want to share one… or maybe not, once you've had a taste!

Folar Algarvio

One of the traditional Portuguese treats from the southernmost region of Algarve is the Folar Algarvio. This rich, sweet bread is a staple around Easter, but you can find and enjoy it all year round in Albufeira and other parts of the Algarve.

Folar Algarvio has a long history and carries a significant cultural symbolism. The recipe for this delectable treat varies from region to region in Portugal, with the Algarve version known for its distinctive ingredients and flavor profile.

Folar Algarvio is a round, doughnut-shaped cake made from sweet dough enriched with eggs, sugar, and infused with aromatic spices like cinnamon and fennel. The dough also contains a generous amount of local dried fruits, such as figs and almonds, enhancing the cake's richness and texture.

One of the most distinctive aspects of Folar Algarvio is its unique preparation method. After shaping the dough, bakers create a small depression in the middle, placing a raw egg (often still in its shell) or a sweet, hard-boiled egg in it. During the baking process, the egg cooks, becoming a signature feature of the cake.

When you cut into a Folar Algarvio, you're met with a rich, moist crumb dotted with dried fruits, a delightful combination of sweet and savory flavors, and the unique surprise of the baked egg. It's perfect for enjoying as breakfast, a snack with a cup of coffee, or even as a dessert.

So, when you're in Albufeira, don't miss out on trying a slice of Folar Algarvio. Whether purchased from a local bakery or sampled as part of an Easter feast, this sweet bread offers a taste of Algarve tradition you won't soon forget.

Doces de Maçapão

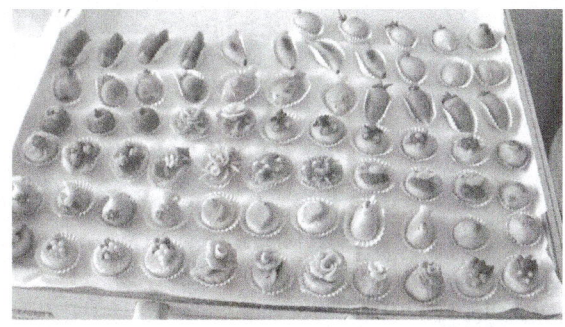

When in Albufeira, indulging in a traditional Portuguese sweet like Doces de Maçapão is a must. The Algarve region, in particular, is renowned for its exceptional variety of almond-based confectioneries, and among them, Doces de Maçapão holds a special place.

Maçapão is a type of marzipan, a sweet, pliable mixture made from ground almonds, sugar, and often a touch of egg white. In Algarve, this almond paste is skillfully crafted into a myriad of whimsical shapes, ranging from fruits, vegetables, and flowers to animals and traditional Portuguese symbols. Each piece is then beautifully hand-painted with food coloring, turning these sweets not only into a delicious treat but also into a piece of edible art.

One of the reasons why Doces de Maçapão are so popular in Algarve is because of the region's abundance of almond trees. As the story goes, the almond trees in the region were introduced by a Moorish king who planted them to please his Nordic wife, who missed the snow. When in bloom, the almond trees with their white flowers would resemble a snowy landscape, and thus remind her of home.

Tasting Doces de Maçapão can be a delightful sensory experience. These sweets have a slightly granular texture, a sweet yet subtly nutty flavor, and a distinctively delicate aroma from the almonds. They are typically enjoyed with a cup of coffee or tea or served as a dessert at the end of a meal.

Visitors to Albufeira can find Doces de Maçapão in many local pastry shops or markets. Some places even offer workshops where you can learn the art of making these marzipan sweets. Trying these treats is not only a way to satisfy your sweet tooth but also a way to partake in the rich gastronomic culture of Algarve.

Algarve's Oranges

The Algarve region in Portugal is world-renowned for its luscious, vibrant oranges, widely considered some of the sweetest and most flavourful globally. These citrus fruits are one of the Algarve's most significant agricultural products and have become a symbol of the region's rich agricultural heritage.

In the Algarve, the cultivation of oranges has been a long-standing tradition. It is believed that the Moors introduced the sweet orange tree during their occupation of the Iberian Peninsula between the 8th and 15th centuries. The favourable Mediterranean climate of the Algarve, with its warm summers and mild winters, along with its fertile soil, creates the perfect conditions for growing oranges.

Walking around Albufeira or anywhere else in the Algarve, you'll frequently see orange trees laden with bright, juicy fruits in gardens, parks, and groves. There's even an annual Orange Festival held in Silves, a town in the Algarve known for its extensive orange groves.

Algarve's oranges are usually harvested between December and May, but due to the region's favourable climate, fresh oranges can be found almost year-round. These oranges have a unique taste profile: incredibly sweet with a slight tang, bursting with juice and extremely aromatic. Their bright and refreshing flavour is a real treat, whether you're enjoying them fresh, in a glass of juice, or as part of a dessert or dish.

Visitors to Albufeira should definitely make a point to sample Algarve's oranges. Whether you're buying them from a local market or sipping on a fresh-squeezed glass of orange juice at a café, you'll be savouring a taste of the Algarve's sunshine in every bite or sip. Plus, these oranges are packed with vitamins and nutrients, making them a healthy and delicious addition to your diet while you explore this beautiful region.

7.2 Seafood in Albufeira

Albufeira is a seafood lover's paradise. Thanks to its prime location along Portugal's southern coastline, Albufeira enjoys a bountiful supply of fresh seafood that forms the cornerstone of its culinary culture. From traditional fishing taverns to fine dining restaurants, Albufeira presents an irresistible spread of seafood delights, reflecting the essence of the Algarve's gastronomy.

Here's a taste of what you can expect from Albufeira's seafood scene:

1. Fresh Fish: Every day, local fishers bring in a range of fish such as sea bass, golden bream, red mullet, and monkfish. These are cooked simply - often grilled over charcoal or baked in the oven - allowing the natural flavors to shine through.

2. Shellfish: Albufeira is famous for its shellfish, including clams, mussels, oysters, and razor clams. "Ameijoas à Bulhão Pato" is a popular local dish of clams cooked in white wine, garlic, and coriander.

3. Crustaceans: Crustaceans, including lobsters, crabs, and prawns, are also abundant in Albufeira. A must-try is the Algarve-style prawns

(Camarão à Algarvia), cooked with garlic, piri-piri sauce, olive oil, and sometimes a dash of white wine.

4. Octopus: Octopus is a local favorite, often appearing in various forms, such as grilled, stewed, or even in salads. "Polvo à Lagareiro" – octopus baked in the oven with punched potatoes, garlic, and olive oil – is a traditional dish that's a favorite among locals and tourists alike.

5. Cataplana: Named after the clam-shaped copper pot it's cooked in, Cataplana is a seafood stew that typically includes a mix of fish and shellfish, along with pork, tomatoes, onions, and herbs. It's a feast for the senses and a must-try when in Albufeira.

Visiting the local markets, such as the Municipal Market of Albufeira (Mercado Municipal de Albufeira), offers a glimpse of the vast array of seafood available in this coastal town. Whether you're a fan of seafood or looking to try something new, Albufeira provides a gastronomic adventure you'll not soon forget.

Remember to pair your seafood with a glass of crisp Vinho Verde or a bottle of Algarve wine to enhance the overall dining experience. With its vibrant seafood culture, Albufeira allows you to savour the ocean's bounty in every meal, making your visit to this charming Portuguese town even more memorable.

7.3 Vegetarian and Vegan Options

While Albufeira is undoubtedly a seafood haven, the city also caters wonderfully to vegetarians and vegans. A rise in plant-based living has seen an increase in restaurants offering vegan and vegetarian dishes, reflecting a modern twist to the traditional Portuguese cuisine.

1. Restaurant Options: Several restaurants, such as Manjua Vegan Kitchen, Bio & Natural Restaurant, and Vegetarianus, provide an exclusively vegetarian or vegan menu. These establishments use fresh, locally sourced ingredients to create dishes that are not only healthy but incredibly delicious. From vegan versions of traditional

Portuguese dishes to creative, internationally inspired cuisine, these eateries offer a wide array of options.

2. Local Dishes: Traditional Portuguese cuisine has several vegetarian dishes like "Sopa Alentejana" (bread and garlic soup), "Açorda" (a bread-based dish with herbs and olive oil), and various salads. For dessert, Algarve's sweet treats like "Dom Rodrigo" and "Doces de Maçapão" (marzipan sweets) are naturally vegetarian.

3. Supermarkets and Health Food Stores: For those who prefer to cook their meals or are looking for plant-based snacks, supermarkets in Albufeira offer a range of vegan and vegetarian products. Health food stores such as Celeiro and Bio-Forma provide organic fruits, vegetables, whole grains, dairy alternatives, and other plant-based products.

4. Farmer's Market: Albufeira's local markets are a great place to find fresh, locally grown produce. The Albufeira Farmers Market (Mercado dos Caliços) is held every Tuesday between 7 am and 1 pm, offering a vast array of fruits, vegetables, nuts, seeds, and more.

5. Vegan Wines: For wine lovers, it's worth noting that not all wines are vegan or vegetarian due to the fining process. However, there are several Portuguese wineries that produce vegan wines. You can find these in local wine shops or inquire at restaurants.

When dining out, don't hesitate to ask the restaurant staff about vegetarian or vegan options. Most chefs will be more than willing to cater to your dietary needs. With growing demand and increased consciousness towards plant-based eating, Albufeira is embracing the shift, ensuring every visitor enjoys a diverse and satisfying culinary journey.

7.4 Street Food and Snacks

Albufeira offers a vibrant street food culture that beautifully represents the Portuguese love for food. These quick bites and snacks are perfect for those on the move, providing a taste of local cuisine in a convenient, casual setting. Here are some must-try street foods and snacks while in Albufeira:

1. Pastel de Nata: One of Portugal's most iconic treats, these custard tarts are creamy, sweet, and encased in a flaky, buttery crust. You can find them in most bakeries or 'pastelerias.' Pair them with a cup of strong Portuguese coffee for a traditional experience.

2. Bifana: This simple yet satisfying sandwich consists of a tender pork cutlet marinated in garlic and spices, served in a fresh bread roll. It's a popular quick meal option available at most street food stalls and local 'tascas' (taverns).

3. Pão com Chouriço: A staple snack, this is essentially a bread roll with chouriço (Portuguese sausage) baked right into it. The result is a delicious, hearty snack perfect for on-the-go.

4. Salgados: These are savory pastries filled with various ingredients like cheese, shrimp, or cod. The most famous one is the "pastel de bacalhau" (codfish cake), but you can also try "rissois" (half-moon shaped pastries) and "coxinha" (chicken croquette).

5. Sardinhas Assadas: In the summer, the smell of grilled sardines fills the streets of Albufeira. Served with a slice of bread, it's a favorite snack of locals and tourists alike.

6. Frango Piri-Piri: While not exactly street food, this spicy grilled chicken is a must-try in Albufeira. There are several "churrasqueiras" (grill houses) in town that serve this delicacy.

7. Fig and Almond Sweets: Often sold at markets and fairs, these traditional Algarve sweets made from dried figs and almonds are delicious and unique to this region.

7.5 Wine and Spirits

Portugal's wines are as diverse and flavorful as its cuisine, and Albufeira, being in the Algarve region, is no exception. The country's distinct geographical and climatic conditions allow the growth of a vast variety of grapes, resulting in a wide range of wines. From full-bodied reds to effervescent whites and everything in between, you'll surely find a wine to suit your palate. Here are some of the local wines and spirits you should consider trying:

1. Vinho Verde: A unique Portuguese wine, Vinho Verde is young, fresh, and slightly fizzy. Although 'verde' translates to 'green,' it refers to the wine being young rather than its color. Vinho Verde is typically white, but there are also red and rosé versions.

2. Algarve Wines: The Algarve region is home to four DOCs (Denominação de Origem Controlada) - Lagos, Portimão, Lagoa, and Tavira, each producing distinct wines. These wines are typically full-bodied, rich, and fruity. Some notable wineries include Quinta da Rosa and Quinta do Francês.

3. Port Wine: Portugal's most famous wine, Port, is a sweet, fortified wine from the Douro Valley in the northern provinces. It comes in several varieties, including white, ruby, tawny, and vintage, each offering a unique tasting experience.

4. Madeira Wine: A fortified wine from the Madeira Islands, Madeira wine is produced in a variety of styles ranging from dry wines that can be consumed on their own or as an aperitif, to sweet wines more usually consumed with dessert.

5. Medronho: A traditional Algarve spirit made from the fruit of the Medronho tree, also known as the Strawberry tree. This potent spirit is traditionally homemade, with many local families in the Algarve region having their own secret recipes.

6. Ginjinha: A popular liqueur in Portugal, made by infusing ginja berries (sour cherry) in alcohol and adding sugar. It's often served in a chocolate cup for an extra treat.

7.6 Dining Etiquette in Albufeira

In Albufeira, dining is not just about the food, but also about enjoying the experience. The Portuguese appreciate good manners and observing local etiquette can enhance your dining experience. Here are some guidelines to follow:

1. Timing: Dinner in Albufeira typically starts a bit later than in some other countries. Restaurants usually start filling up around 8:00 PM and can stay busy until late in the evening. Lunch can also be a leisurely affair, often starting at 1:00 PM and lasting until 3:00 PM.

2. Dress code: Dress codes vary depending on the restaurant. While casual attire is accepted in most places, upscale restaurants may require more formal attire. Check the restaurant's website or call ahead if you're unsure.

3. Tipping: Tipping is customary in Albufeira, but not mandatory. A tip of around 10% is appreciated for good service. However, check your bill first, as some restaurants include a service charge.

4. Table manners: The Portuguese value good table manners. Keep your elbows off the table, use your utensils correctly, and remember to say "Bom apetite" (Enjoy your meal) before you start eating.

5. Ordering: When ordering, it's common to start with a "couvert" (a set of appetizers such as bread, butter, olives), followed by a starter (entrada), then the main course (prato principal), and finally dessert (sobremesa). Note that the couvert is not free and will be added to your bill.

6. Wine: If you order wine, the waiter may present the bottle for you to inspect. This is simply a traditional ritual where you confirm it is the wine you ordered. They will then pour a little for you to taste.

7. Asking for the bill: In Albufeira, as in most parts of Portugal, the waiter will not bring the bill until you ask for it. It's considered rude to rush customers. So, when you're ready, ask for "a conta, por favor" (the bill, please).

8. Patience: The Portuguese approach to dining is relaxed and unhurried. Service might be slower compared to other countries, but it's part of the local dining culture meant to savor the meal and the company.

7.7 Top Rated Restaurants

Albufeira boasts an abundance of dining options that range from traditional Portuguese eateries to fine-dining establishments. Here are some top-rated restaurants in Albufeira that you should consider during your visit:

1. Vila Joya: This two Michelin-starred restaurant offers a menu full of local, fresh ingredients and inventive dishes inspired by the sea. The beautiful setting overlooking the Atlantic Ocean and the superb wine list make it a perfect place for a special occasion. Advance booking is recommended. You can book a table here.

2. O Marinheiro: This Portuguese restaurant located near the Salgados Beach is famous for its seafood dishes and its cataplana. The relaxed atmosphere and excellent service add to the dining experience. You can find more information here.

3. Dom Carlos Restaurant: This small, intimate restaurant located in the heart of Albufeira offers a daily changing five-course gourmet menu based on local ingredients. The owner, Carlos, adds a personal touch to the service. Check it out here.

4. Casa do Avô: With a history dating back to 1981, this restaurant offers Portuguese cuisine and a selection of locally sourced wines. The lamb stew and the black pig are must-try dishes. For more information, click here.

5. Cabana Fresca Restaurant: Located on the Fisherman's Beach, it offers traditional Portuguese seafood and meat dishes. The view of the beach is stunning, and the food is consistently high quality. More information is available here.

6. Os Arcos Restaurante: This family-run restaurant located in the old town of Albufeira specializes in traditional Portuguese cuisine. You can expect a variety of fresh fish and seafood dishes at this local gem. Visit their website for more.

7. Al Quimia: Located in the EPIC SANA Algarve Hotel, this fine-dining restaurant offers modern Portuguese cuisine in an elegant setting. The tasting menu is a great way to experience the chef's creativity. Find more information here.

Remember to check opening times and book in advance where necessary, especially during the peak season. Enjoy your culinary journey in Albufeira!

8. Shopping in Albufeira

Albufeira offers an exciting range of shopping experiences. From modern shopping centers and charming local markets to specialty and gift shops filled with unique treasures, you will have a lot to explore.

8.1 Shopping Centers and Malls

Algarve Shopping Mall: Located in Guia, just a few kilometers from Albufeira, this is one of the largest shopping centers in the region. It houses a variety of shops selling clothing, electronics, cosmetics, and more, as well as a large food court and a cinema. Check out their website here for more information.

Marina de Albufeira: While primarily a marina, this area also has a number of shops selling everything from beachwear to souvenirs. Its colorful buildings and scenic waterfront make it a pleasant place to stroll and shop.

8.2 Local Markets

Municipal Market of Albufeira (Mercado Municipal de Albufeira): Open from Monday to Saturday, this is a great place to find fresh local produce, fish, meat, and a variety of Algarvean specialties.

Gypsy Market: Held in different locations in Albufeira on different days of the week, this market is perfect for those looking for unique bargains. You'll find clothing, crafts, handbags, and an array of other items.

8.3 Specialty and Gift Shops

Portugal's Memories: Located near the old town of Albufeira, this shop sells a wide range of Portuguese souvenirs and crafts. It's a great place to buy ceramics, cork products, and traditional Portuguese items.

Cork World: A unique store selling items made from cork, a sustainable material widely grown in Portugal. From bags and accessories to home decor, it's an ideal spot to find eco-friendly and distinctive gifts.

Maria's Algarve: This charming shop offers high-quality hand-painted ceramics and pottery. Each piece is unique, making this a great place to find a special memento of your visit to Albufeira.

8.4 Buying Souvenirs

Portuguese souvenirs offer a delightful mix of tradition and creativity. From hand-painted ceramics and delicate filigree jewelry to locally produced wines and olive oils, there's a treasure to suit every taste.

In Albufeira, check out the *Old Town* area for a range of souvenir shops, offering a variety of local products. Consider buying Portuguese ceramics, traditional cork products, or beautifully woven textiles.

For foodie gifts, look out for local produce such as Algarvian honey, olive oils, or a bottle of the famous Portuguese Port wine or Vinho Verde. Sweet treats like pastéis de nata (custard tarts) are also popular take-home gifts.

8.5 Portuguese Crafts and Textiles

Portugal has a rich tradition of handicrafts and textiles.

Ceramics: Portuguese ceramics are renowned for their beauty and quality. The town of Porches, near Albufeira, is famous for its pottery. You can find beautifully painted dishes, bowls, and tiles here.

Cork Products: Portugal is the world's largest cork producer. You'll find a variety of items made from this sustainable material, including handbags, shoes, and home decor items.

Embroidery: The regions of Madeira and Minho are known for their intricate embroidery work. You can buy tablecloths, napkins, and even clothing featuring this beautiful handiwork.

Arraiolos Rugs: These handcrafted wool rugs are named after the town of Arraiolos in central Portugal. They are hand embroidered with designs that date back to the Middle Ages.

Linen and Lace: Portuguese linens are highly regarded. The regions of Guimarães and Viana do Castelo are known for producing high-quality bed linens, tablecloths, and towels.

Portuguese Soaps: Portugal has a long history of producing luxurious soaps infused with fragrances from the region's flowers and herbs.

When buying Portuguese crafts and textiles, look for products labeled "Handmade in Portugal" to ensure you are purchasing authentic local products.

9. Seasonal Events and Festivals

9.1 Music Festivals

Albufeira hosts a variety of music festivals throughout the year, catering to different musical tastes:

Festival Med: Usually held in June in nearby Loulé, this festival celebrates music from the Mediterranean and beyond. It features multiple stages with music ranging from Fado, Samba, Flamenco, and much more.

Albufeira Summer Live: A free open-air concert series held during July and August in the Old Town Square. The festival showcases a mix of Portuguese and international artists.

Al-Buhera Festival: This five-day festival in July is held by the seaside in Albufeira and, along with music, offers a craft fair and gastronomic delights.

9.2 Traditional Portuguese Festivals

Festa do Pescador (Fishermen's Festival): Celebrated in September, this festival is dedicated to Albufeira's fishing community. It features folk music, traditional dances, and plenty of seafood.

Carnaval: Like the rest of Portugal, Albufeira celebrates Carnaval in February or March with a colourful street parade and parties throughout the town.

Festa de São João (St. John's Festival): Celebrated in June, this is one of the biggest festivals in Portugal. In Albufeira, locals celebrate with street parties, traditional dances, and bonfires.

Festa da Nossa Senhora da Orada (Our Lady of Orada Festival): Held in August, this religious festival is dedicated to the patron saint of fishermen. It includes a procession to the sea and a vibrant fireworks display.

Christmas and New Year: Albufeira is known for its elaborate Christmas light display and festive atmosphere. For New Year's Eve, there is a spectacular fireworks display and concerts held in the main square.

These events offer an excellent opportunity to immerse yourself in the local culture, taste traditional Portuguese food and enjoy the festive atmosphere. Be sure to check the exact dates as they can change from year to year.

9.3 Sports Events

Albufeira is a hub for various sports events throughout the year, attracting local and international participants:

Algarve Cup: An international women's football tournament held annually in March. Games are played in various cities across the Algarve, including Albufeira.

Cross Internacional das Amendoeiras: This international cross country race takes place in February and is part of the IAAF Cross Country Permit Meetings series.

Albufeira Golf Open: Golfers from around the world gather in Albufeira for this tournament, usually held in October at one of the region's top golf courses.

Algarve Classic Cars: An annual vintage car rally held in July, with Albufeira being one of the main stages.

9.4 Art and Film Festivals

Art and culture are deeply rooted in Albufeira. Some of the town's most renowned art and film festivals include:

Algarve International Film Festival: Usually held in May, it's one of the oldest film events in Portugal. It showcases a selection of independent films from around the world.

Albufeira Art Festival: A biannual event, held in the summer and winter, that exhibits the work of local and international artists across various mediums. It includes live performances, workshops, and art installations throughout the city.

Sand City FIESA: Not exactly a festival, but a remarkable art exhibit nonetheless. It's the largest sand sculpture exhibition in the world, held from March to November in nearby Pêra.

Albufeira New Year's Eve Sculpture Symposium: During December, artists create sculptures throughout the town that are then lit up to ring in the New Year.

For all these events, it is recommended to check their official websites or local tourist information centers for the latest updates and schedules.

10. Essential Information

10.1 Safety and Security

Albufeira is generally a safe destination for tourists. However, like any travel destination, it's important to remain vigilant, especially in crowded areas. There can be occasional petty crimes like pickpocketing, especially during peak tourist seasons. Also, avoid deserted areas at night and always keep your belongings secure.

Local police, known as 'Policia,' are available to assist in case of emergencies. The emergency contact number in Portugal is 112.

10.2 Health and Medical Services

The public health care system in Portugal is generally of high standard. In Albufeira, there are several public and private clinics, pharmacies, and a hospital (Hospital Lusiadas Albufeira). Travel insurance that covers medical expenses is highly recommended. In case of emergency, dial 112.

10.3 Money and Banking

The official currency of Portugal is the Euro (€). ATMs, known as 'Multibanco,' are widely available. Credit cards are accepted in most places, but it's always wise to carry some cash, particularly for smaller establishments or rural areas.

10.4 Local Laws and Customs

Portugal is a friendly country with a laid-back lifestyle. However, remember to respect local customs. Noise restrictions are in place from 11 pm to 7 am. Smoking is banned in public enclosed spaces. The legal drinking age is 18.

10.5 Useful Phrases and Language Tips

While English is commonly spoken in tourist areas, it's appreciated if you try to speak some Portuguese phrases.

Here are a few useful ones:

- Hello: Olá
- Goodbye: Adeus
- Please: Por favor
- Thank you: Obrigado (if you're a man), Obrigada (if you're a woman)

- Good morning! – Bom dia!
- Good afternoon! – Boa tarde!
- Good evening! – Boa noite!
- Welcome to Portugal! – Bem-vindo/a a Portugal!
- Thank you! – Obrigado/a![2]
- I'm very thankful! – Eu estou muito agradecido/a!
- Appreciated! – Agradecido/a!
- You're welcome! – De nada!
- Nice to meet you! – Prazer em conhecê-lo/a!
- My name is ... – O meu nome é ...
- How are you? – Como está?
- And you? – E o/a senhor(a)?
- Hello! – Olá!
- Hi! – Oi!
- Thank your for your help! – Obrigado/a pela sua ajuda.
- It was a pleasure to meet you! – Foi um prazer conhecê-lo/a.
- Best regards. – Melhores cumprimentos.
- See you soon! – Até já!
- See you later! – Até logo!
- See you tomorrow! – Até amanhã!
- Give me a hug! – Dê-me um abraço!
- Give me a kiss![3] – Dê-me um beijo!
- Handshake. – Mãozada/Passou bem.
- Goodbye! – Adeus!
- Bye! – Xau!

- Do you speak English? – Fala Inglês?
- I only speak English. – Eu só falo Inglês.
- I don't speak Portuguese very well. – Eu não falo Português muito bem.
- I need some help. – Eu preciso de ajuda.
- What did you say? – O que disse?
- Can you repeat that, please? – Pode repetir, por favor?
- Can you translate for me? – Pode traduzir para mim?
- Could you speak more slowly, please? – Podia falar mais devagar, por favor?
- One more time. – Mais uma vez.
- What does that mean? – O que significa isso?
- How do you say this in Portuguese? – Como se diz isto em Português?
- How do you say that in English? – Como se diz isso em Inglês?
- How do you spell it? – Como se soletra?
- I understand. – Eu percebo/entendo.
- I don't understand. – Não percebo/entendo.
- Could you write that down, please? – Pode escrever isso, por favor?
- Do you speak English? – Fala Inglês?
- I'm lost. – Estou perdido/a.
- Can you help me, please? – Pode ajudar-me, por favor?
- Just a moment. – Um momento.
- Yes. – Sim.
- No. – Não.
- This. – Isto.
- That. – Aquilo/Aquele/a.
- Those. – Aqueles/as.
- These. – Estes/as.
- Where is the bathroom. – Onde é a casa de banho?
- I'm sorry. – Lamento/Desculpe.
- Excuse me. – Com licença/Desculpe.
- Please. – Por favor.
- I'm ... years old. – Eu tenho ... anos.
- Is everything ok? – Está tudo bem?
- Everything is great! – Está tudo bem.
- I'm fine! – Estou bem!
- Let's go! – Vamos!
- No problem. – Sem problema/Não há problema.

- Ok. – Ok.
- Sure. – Claro/Com certeza.
- Where is the entrance – Onde é a entrada?
- It's open. – Está aberto.
- It's closed. – Está fechado.
- Danger! – Perigo!
- Watch out! – Cuidado!
- It's an emergency. – É uma emergência.
- It's urgent. – É urgente.
- Please, hurry. – Por favor, despache-se.
- No exit here. – Não há saída aqui.
- Ladies and gentlemen. – Senhoras e senhores.
- Mr. – Senhor
- Mrs. – Senhora
- Man – Homem
- Woman – Mulher

Tip 1:It is very common in many countries throughout Europe to give kisses when greeting or saying goodbye. In Portugal, people exchange two kisses, one for each cheek. However, if it is a formal situation you can just give a handshake. Generally, Portuguese are very caring and warm people, so get used to more touches and hugs when you get more comfortable and familiar with a native!

Tip 2:You should say «Obrigado» if you are a man, and «Obrigada» if you are a woman. It does not depend on whoever you are saying it to.

Tip 3: A good way to start any conversation and to make everyone you meet instantly like you, is to start every sentence with a greeting, such as «Olá/Oi» (Hello/Hi!) or « Bom dia!» (Good morning), or even «Desculpe!» (Excuse me!), instead of going straight to what you want to say; and always end it with «por favor/se faz favor» (please) or «se não se importa» (if you don't mind), and a «Obrigado/a» (Thank you). Especially in Portugal, manners and politeness are very much appreciated, so those few details will help you start out elegantly. A good tip to graciously start any conversation and to make everyone you meet instantly like you, is to start every sentence with a greeting, such as «Olá/Oi» (Hello/Hi!) or « Bom dia!» (Good morning), or even «Desculpe!» (Excuse me!), instead of going straight to what you want to say; and always end it with «por favor/se faz favor» (please) or «se não se importa» (if you don't mind), and a «Obrigado/a» (Thank you). Especially in Portugal, manners and politeness are very much appreciated, so those few details will help you start out elegantly.

10.6 Weather and Clothing Tips

Albufeira, like the rest of the Algarve, boasts a Mediterranean climate characterized by long, warm to hot summers and mild, occasionally rainy winters. The city enjoys abundant sunshine throughout the year, averaging around 300 sunny days annually.

During the **summer months (June to September)**, temperatures can rise above 30°C (86°F). Therefore, it is advisable to pack lightweight, breathable clothing, a wide-brimmed hat, sunglasses, and a high SPF sunblock. Don't forget your swimsuit for those refreshing beach days.

The **spring (March to May) and autumn (October and November)** months in Albufeira are pleasantly warm, with average temperatures hovering between 15-25°C (59-77°F). Packing a light jacket or sweater is a good idea for cooler evenings, and as always, bring sun protection.

Winter (December to February) sees mild temperatures ranging between 8°C to 16°C (46°F to 61°F). While the Algarve is one of the warmest regions in Portugal during winter, it's wise to pack warmer clothes like coats, jackets, and sweaters for cooler days and nights. This is also the wettest time of year, so an umbrella or waterproof coat could come in handy.

Regardless of the season, if you're planning to visit religious sites such as churches, remember to dress modestly. It's also worth noting that many Portuguese restaurants and establishments appreciate a smart-casual dress code in the evenings.

10.7 Frequently Asked Questions

Where to Stay in Albufeira to Party?

If you're looking for a lively party scene, there are two main areas to consider in Albufeira. For a balance between nightlife and a family-friendly atmosphere, downtown in the Old Town is a great option. Here, you'll find numerous bars and entertainment venues that cater to different tastes. A recommended hotel in this area is the Hotel Sol e Mar, available from 75€ per night. Alternatively, if you prefer a more energetic and bustling nightlife experience, staying near The Strip in the New Town is the way to go. This area is known for its frenetic bars and nightclubs that stay open late until dawn. Hotel da Aldeia is a popular choice in this location, available from 51€ per night.

Where to Stay in Albufeira on Honeymoon?

For a memorable honeymoon experience, Albufeira offers some romantic and luxurious resorts that will enhance your special moments. One option is the Epic Sana Hotels Algarve, offering breathtaking views of Falésia Beach and featuring a fantastic restaurant called Alquimia. Prices for this resort start from 192€ per night. Another excellent choice is the Pine Cliffs Resort Algarve, which boasts stunning views of Santa Eulália Beach and houses the Japanese fusion restaurant, Yakuza. Prices for this resort start from 234€ per night. While the prices may be higher, these exceptional resorts provide an unforgettable setting for your honeymoon, ensuring a truly magical experience.

Should I use Airbnb to stay in Albufeira?

If you're planning to visit Albufeira during the summertime, it's important to note that prices for Airbnb options tend to be very high. This is due to the high demand and popularity of the destination during peak season. However, if you're considering visiting Albufeira during other times of the year, Airbnb can be a great choice, offering a variety of accommodation options to suit your needs. To explore available Airbnb listings in Albufeira, you can visit the Airbnb Albufeira website.

Can I find a fantastic hotel with 50€ per night in Albufeira?

Finding a fantastic hotel in Albufeira for 50€ per night can be quite challenging, especially during the peak months of June, July, August, and September. During these busy periods, it's recommended to budget between 70€ and 120€ per night for a decent double room in a hotel. This price range will ensure that you have a comfortable stay with good amenities and services. It's advisable to book your hotel in advance to secure the best available rates and options that fit within your budget.

Where are Albufeira's best views?

There are many spots to watch the breathtaking views or to relax and have a look at the setting sun on the horizon. Check out this link that shows the main spots in Albufeira: **Best Views**

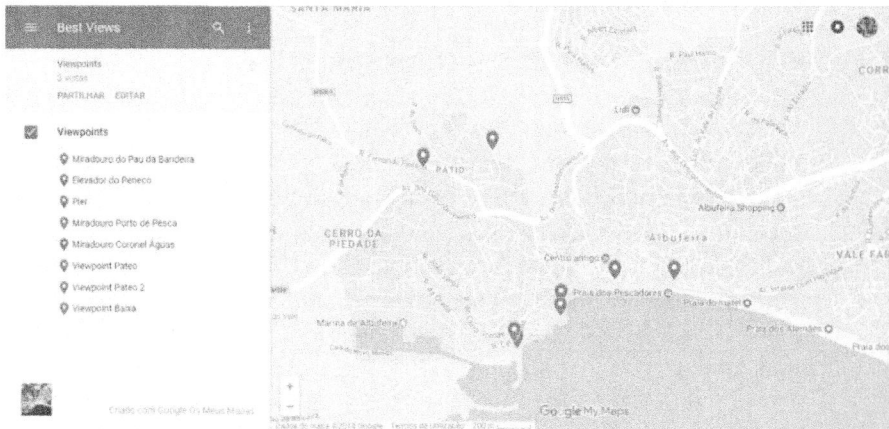

Car Parking for Rent-a-Car:

It's important to consider car parking options for your rented car in Albufeira. Given the high number of visitors during the summer, finding parking can sometimes be a challenge and consume valuable time. Therefore, it's recommended to check if your hotel, restaurant, or the area you're staying in provides a parking area for your convenience. This way, you can ensure the safety and accessibility of your rental car while exploring the city.

Booking Hotels in Advance:

If you plan to visit Albufeira during the peak months, particularly the high season, it's advisable to book your hotel at least two months in advance. By doing so, you'll have a better chance of securing an excellent price for a nice hotel. Albufeira boasts a wide range of accommodation options, and even during the busiest times, you'll likely find a place to stay. However, last-minute bookings or delayed reservations may result in higher prices or limited availability, potentially compromising the quality of your accommodation.

Busiest Months in Albufeira:

The months of June, July, August, and September are undeniably the busiest and most bustling in Albufeira. During this time, the city experiences a surge in tourists and an energetic atmosphere. However, it's worth noting that Albufeira welcomes visitors starting from May and extends its tourism season until late October. While the city's vibrancy may decline during the winter months, with many restaurants closing and a less dynamic nightlife scene, Albufeira remains a popular destination for those seeking a tranquil coastal retreat during the off-peak season.

Local Visitation in Albufeira:

Portuguese locals tend to visit Albufeira during the months of June, July, August, and September. These are the months when many locals take their own vacations and escape to the beautiful beaches and lively atmosphere of Albufeira. If you're looking to experience a mix of local and international visitors, these months offer a vibrant and dynamic environment.

Best Time for Swimming in Albufeira:

For optimal swimming conditions, the period from May to late September is the best time to enjoy the warm waters of Albufeira. During these months, the water temperature is pleasantly warm, allowing for comfortable swimming and various water activities. However, even outside of this period, it is still possible to take a refreshing swim in the ocean, although the water might be slightly colder. With that said, it's always a good idea to check the current water conditions and exercise caution when swimming during the cooler months.

10.8 Top Things to do in Albufeira

Albufeira offers a wide variety of fun things to do, and we compiled a list of the most exciting activities to try in Albufeira that are not in the 3-day guide. You can, with any trouble or hassle, switch any of the activities proposed on the guide for one of these, provided you account for the different distances, time spent, scheduling/planning and booking matters.

In Albufeira:

- Go on the Turistren, the tourist train that goes around Albufeira. Click here to see a preview: Turistren Preview;

- Hop on one of several Tuk Tuk's – a mean of transport popular in India and Thailand, that now roams around Albufeira on arranged tours;

- Go on a Jeep Safari tour and adventure through the picturesque views of Algarve!;

- Do water activities, like Scuba Diving; Stand up Paddle; Surf; Parasailing; Jet-ski;
- Kayak Tours; Coasteering, and many more;

- Try to speed things up and ride a kart!;

- Visit Parque Aventura, to do activities like paintball, horse-riding;

- Visit the water park Aqualand; Slide&Splash; or Aquashow;

- If you like golf, then you can visit Pine Cliffs Golf Course;

- Or maybe experience a fishing trip - Beach Fishing Tours.

10.9 The Best Tours to Book in Albufeira

Here is the information on the best tours to book while you are in Albufeira. The best site to book your tours and get some decent discounts is Get Your Guide.

Click on the following link to find out the best tours in Albufeira: Best Tours in Albufeira

11. Day Trips from Albufeira

11.1 Lagos

If you're looking to explore beyond Albufeira, a day trip to Lagos is highly recommended. Located about 50 kilometers west of Albufeira, Lagos is a picturesque town known for its stunning coastline, historic sites, and charming old town. Here's a suggested daily itinerary to make the most of your day trip:

Morning:

- Depart from Albufeira to Lagos (approximately 1-hour drive).

- Start your day by visiting the **Ponta da Piedade**, a stunning natural rock formation with breathtaking cliffs and turquoise waters. You can take a boat tour to explore the caves and grottos or simply enjoy the view from the top. Boat tours usually cost around €20 per person.

- After the boat tour, head to the **Lagos Marina** and enjoy a leisurely stroll along the waterfront, lined with shops, restaurants, and cafes.

Mid-day:

- Continue to the **Lagos Old Town** and visit the **Church of Saint Anthony**. This beautiful church dates back to the 18th century and features intricate Baroque architecture.

- Take a walk through the **historic city center**, where you can admire the charming narrow streets, colorful buildings, and local shops. Don't miss the opportunity to explore the local market, **Mercado de Escravos**, where you can find fresh produce and traditional products.

- For lunch, indulge in delicious seafood dishes at one of the local restaurants in the old town. Prices can vary depending on the restaurant, but a typical meal can range from €15 to €30 per person.

Afternoon:

- Head to the famous **Meia Praia Beach**, located just outside the city center. This long stretch of golden sand offers plenty of space to relax and soak up the sun. You can also try various water sports activities such as kayaking or paddleboarding. Rental prices for water sports equipment can range from €15 to €30 per hour.

- If you're interested in history, visit the **Lagos Slave Market**, a historic building that once served as the first slave market in Europe. The entrance fee is €4 for adults.

- End your day with a visit to the **Lagos Fortress** (Fortaleza da Ponta da Bandeira), a 17th-century fortress that offers stunning views of the coastline. The entrance fee is €4 for adults.

Evening:

- Enjoy a relaxing walk along the **Lagos Promenade** and soak in the beautiful sunset views.

- Before heading back to Albufeira, indulge in a delicious dinner at one of the many restaurants in Lagos. Prices can vary depending on the restaurant and your chosen dishes, but expect to spend around €20 to €40 per person for a meal.

Note: The suggested itinerary is flexible, and you can adjust the timing and activities based on your preferences. It's always recommended to check the opening hours and availability of attractions and restaurants in advance.

11.2 Faro

If you're interested in exploring the capital city of the Algarve, a day trip to Faro is a fantastic choice. With its historic center, cultural attractions, and vibrant atmosphere, Faro offers a delightful blend of history and modernity. Here's a suggested daily itinerary for your day trip to Faro:

Morning:

- Depart from Albufeira to Faro (approximately 40-minute drive or take a train from Albufeira-Ferreiras station to Faro).

- Start your day by visiting the **Faro Old Town**, also known as Cidade Velha. Explore the **Arco da Vila**, an ancient gate that leads to the historic center. From there, take a walk along the charming cobbled streets lined with traditional houses, shops, and cafes.

- Visit the **Faro Cathedral** (Se de Faro), a beautiful 13th-century cathedral located in the heart of the old town. Admire the stunning architecture and climb the tower for panoramic views of the city. The entrance fee is usually around €3 per person.

Mid-day:

- Enjoy a delicious lunch at one of the traditional restaurants in Faro. The old town offers a variety of options, including local seafood dishes, traditional Portuguese cuisine, and international flavors. Prices can range from €10 to €30 per person, depending on the restaurant.

Afternoon:

- Take a boat tour to explore the **Ria Formosa Natural Park**, a stunning coastal lagoon system that stretches along the Algarve coast. These boat tours offer an opportunity to observe the diverse flora and fauna of the area. Prices vary depending on the duration and type of tour, but expect to pay around €20 to €30 per person.

- Visit the **Carmo Church and Bones Chapel** (Igreja do Carmo e Capela dos Ossos). This unique attraction features a chapel entirely decorated with human bones, creating a fascinating and somewhat macabre ambiance. The entrance fee is usually around €2 per person.

Evening:

- Explore the **Marina de Faro**, a modern marina area with a bustling atmosphere, waterfront restaurants, and shops. Enjoy a refreshing drink or indulge in a seafood dinner while taking in the views of the boats and the Ria Formosa.

- Take a leisurely walk along the **Faro Promenade** and enjoy the picturesque sunset over the Ria Formosa.

- Before returning to Albufeira, don't miss the opportunity to sample some traditional Portuguese pastries, such as **pasteis de nata** (custard tarts), at a local bakery.

11.3 Tavira

A day trip to Tavira is a must for those seeking a charming and historic destination. Located along the eastern coast of the Algarve, Tavira is known for its picturesque streets, ancient architecture, and beautiful beaches. Here's a suggested daily itinerary for your day trip to Tavira:

Morning:

- Depart from Albufeira to Tavira (approximately 1-hour drive).

- Begin your day by exploring the **Tavira Castle** (Castelo de Tavira) and the **Tavira Tower** (Torre de Tavira). Climb the tower for panoramic views of the city and the Gilão River. The entrance fee is usually around €3 per person.

- Take a leisurely stroll through the **Roman Bridge** (Ponte Romana) and explore the charming streets of the historic center. Admire the traditional houses, narrow alleys, and beautiful churches.

Mid-day:

- Enjoy a delicious lunch at one of the local restaurants in Tavira. The town offers a variety of dining options, including traditional

Portuguese cuisine and fresh seafood dishes. Prices can range from €10 to €30 per person, depending on the restaurant.

Afternoon:

- Visit the **Tavira Municipal Market** (Mercado Municipal de Tavira) to experience the local atmosphere and find a variety of fresh produce, local products, and traditional crafts.

- Explore the **Tavira Gran Plaza Mall**, located just outside the town center. This modern shopping mall offers a range of stores, including clothing, accessories, and electronics.

Optional:

- Take a short boat trip to **Ilha de Tavira**, a stunning barrier island with pristine beaches and crystal-clear waters. Enjoy sunbathing, swimming, or simply taking a leisurely walk along the shoreline. Boat transfers to the island usually cost around €2 to €3 per person each way.

- Visit the **Tavira Municipal Museum** (Museu Municipal de Tavira), housed in the 16th-century Convento da Graça. The museum showcases archaeological artifacts and exhibits that highlight the history and culture of the region. The entrance fee is typically around €3 per person.

Evening:

- After returning from Ilha de Tavira or visiting the museum, take some time to relax in one of the many cafes or bars along the **Ribeira Square** (Praça da República). Enjoy a refreshing drink or a cup of Portuguese coffee while soaking up the lively atmosphere.

- Before heading back to Albufeira, savor a traditional Portuguese dinner at one of the local restaurants in Tavira. Prices can vary depending on the restaurant and your chosen dishes, but expect to spend around €20 to €40 per person for a meal.

11.4 Silves

A day trip to Silves, the former capital of the Algarve, promises a journey back in time with its rich history and well-preserved medieval charm. Here's a suggested daily itinerary for your day trip to Silves:

Morning:

- Depart from Albufeira to Silves (approximately 30-minute drive).

- Begin your day by visiting the **Silves Castle** (Castelo de Silves), an impressive Moorish fortress perched atop a hill. Explore the castle's walls, towers, and enjoy panoramic views of the surrounding countryside. The entrance fee is usually around €3 per person.

- Take a stroll through the narrow streets of the historic center and immerse yourself in the medieval atmosphere. Admire the traditional whitewashed houses, quaint shops, and picturesque squares.

Mid-day:

- Enjoy a leisurely lunch at one of the local restaurants in Silves, where you can savor traditional Portuguese cuisine and regional dishes. Prices can range from €10 to €30 per person, depending on the restaurant.

Afternoon:

- Visit the **Silves Cathedral** (Sé Catedral de Silves), a beautiful Gothic-style cathedral with elements of Moorish architecture. Explore the interior, including the cloisters and chapels, and appreciate the stunning craftsmanship. The entrance fee is typically around €2 to €3 per person.

- Discover the **Silves Municipal Market** (Mercado Municipal de Silves), where you can find a variety of fresh produce, local products, and handicrafts. Experience the vibrant atmosphere and interact with local vendors.

- Explore the **Museu Municipal de Arqueologia de Silves**, located near the castle. This archaeological museum showcases artifacts and exhibits that tell the story of Silves' ancient past. The entrance fee is usually around €3 per person.

Optional:

- If you're interested in gardens and nature, take a short drive to the **Silves Riverside Park** (Parque Urbano de Silves), where you can enjoy a peaceful walk along the river and relax amidst beautiful greenery.

- Alternatively, consider a boat trip along the **Arade River**, which offers scenic views of the surrounding countryside and the chance to spot local wildlife. Boat tour prices can vary depending on the duration and type of tour.

Evening:

- Before heading back to Albufeira, stop by one of the local cafes or pastry shops to indulge in a traditional Portuguese dessert, such as **pastel de nata** (custard tart) or **doce fino** (almond pastry).

- Reflect on your day in Silves as you make your way back to Albufeira, taking with you the memories of this historic gem.

11.5 Loulé

A day trip to Loulé offers a delightful blend of history, culture, and traditional markets. Known for its charming old town and vibrant market scene, Loulé is a wonderful destination to explore. Here's a suggested daily itinerary for your day trip to Loulé:

Morning:

- Depart from Albufeira to Loulé (approximately 30-minute drive).

- Start your day by visiting the **Loulé Municipal Market** (Mercado Municipal de Loulé), a bustling market filled with stalls selling fresh produce, local delicacies, and traditional crafts. Take your time to explore the market and soak up the lively atmosphere.

- Next, head to the **Loulé Castle** (Castelo de Loulé), located in the heart of the old town. Although the castle is in ruins, it offers panoramic views of the city and the surrounding countryside. Take a leisurely walk around the castle grounds and imagine the history that once unfolded within its walls.

Mid-day:

Enjoy a leisurely lunch at one of the local restaurants in Loulé, where you can sample traditional Portuguese dishes and regional specialties. Prices can range from €10 to €30 per person, depending on the restaurant.

Afternoon:

- Explore the charming **Loulé Old Town**, with its narrow streets, white-washed houses, and decorative tiles. Admire the beautiful architecture, including the **Igreja de São Clemente**, a 13th-century church known for its azulejo tiles and intricate interior.

- Visit the **Loulé Municipal Museum** (Museu Municipal de Loulé), housed in a restored 18th-century palace. The museum exhibits a collection of archaeological artifacts, traditional crafts, and historical objects. The entrance fee is usually around €2 to €3 per person.

Optional:

- If you're visiting on a Saturday, don't miss the **Saturday Market** (Feira de Loulé), one of the largest and most vibrant markets in the Algarve. Explore the stalls selling fresh produce, clothing, handicrafts, and more. Immerse yourself in the bustling atmosphere and experience the local culture.

- Take a short drive to the nearby **Quarteira Beach** for a relaxing afternoon by the sea. Enjoy the golden sands, take a dip in the crystal-clear waters, or simply unwind and soak up the sun.

Evening:

- Before heading back to Albufeira, treat yourself to a refreshing drink or a cup of coffee at one of the cafes in Loulé. Sit back, relax, and reflect on the day's adventures.

- As you make your way back to Albufeira, take in the beautiful scenery and cherish the memories of your time in Loulé.

3-Day Travel Itinerary to Albufeira

1st Day in Albufeira

07:00am – Arrival at the Faro International Airport.

Image 5 - Faro Airport

07:30am – At 7:30 am, retrieve your bags from the baggage claim area and make your way to the rental car service. The airport in Albufeira is relatively small, so the process of collecting your bags should be quick and efficient. However, it's important to note that during the peak months, the airport can become quite busy with increased traffic and larger crowds. As a result, there may be longer lines and waiting times at the rental car service. It's advisable to allow for some extra time and exercise patience during these periods.

08:00am – At 8:00 am, head to one of the car rental stands at the airport to rent a car for a three-day period. Renting a car provides you with the flexibility and convenience to explore Albufeira and its surrounding areas at your own pace. You can find a variety of car rental options at Faro Airport by visiting this link: https://en.aeroportodefaro.com/car-hire. This website provides detailed information about the available car rental companies, their services, and booking options. Take your time to choose a reliable rental company that suits your needs and preferences. Once you've rented a car, you're ready to embark on your Albufeira adventure with the freedom to discover the region's hidden gems and scenic beauty.

08:30am – If you need, exchange your currency to Euros(€) at Unicâmbio.

09:00am – Get your car and get going. Head to Balaia Mar Hotel.

At 9:00 am, pick up your rental car and begin your journey to the Balaia Mar Hotel. Enjoy the convenience of having your own transportation as you make your way to your accommodation.

09:45am – Arrive at the Balaia Mar Hotel. Check in at the reception. Unpack your bags.

10:30am – Drive to Castle of Paderne.

Around 10:30 am, embark on a scenic drive to the Castle of Paderne. Enjoy the picturesque landscapes and immerse yourself in the rich history of the region.

11:00am – Arrive at Castle of Paderne.

By 11:00 am, you will have arrived at the Castle of Paderne. Take your time to explore this ancient Moorish castle, known for its impressive architecture and historical significance. Enjoy the panoramic views from the castle and learn about its fascinating past.

Image 6 - A gate in the Castle of Paderne

The Castle of Paderne is a historic fortress situated in Albufeira, dating back to the 12th century. It holds great significance as it is considered one of the original castles depicted on the shield of the Portuguese national flag. This well-preserved castle stands as a testament to the region's rich history and offers visitors a glimpse into the past.

As you explore the Castle of Paderne, you'll be captivated by its medieval architecture and strategic position atop a hill. Take your time to wander through its ancient walls, towers, and courtyards, imagining the stories and events that unfolded within its walls centuries ago. The panoramic views from the castle offer a picturesque backdrop of the surrounding countryside.

Additionally, while visiting the Castle of Paderne, take the opportunity to stroll around the nearby Roman bridge. This Roman-era structure adds another layer of historical significance to the area and provides a charming setting for a leisurely walk. Immerse yourself in the atmosphere and appreciate the blend of ancient Roman and medieval Portuguese heritage.

Exploring the Castle of Paderne and the Roman bridge is a memorable experience that allows you to delve into the captivating history and architectural beauty of the region. Don't miss the chance to visit these remarkable landmarks during your time in Albufeira.

Image 7 - Roman Bridge

The Bridge of Paderne, often referred to as the "Roman Bridge," is located near the Castle of Paderne, spanning across the Quarteira River. This historic bridge is believed to have been constructed to serve the castle and its surrounding area.

The Bridge of Paderne, despite its name, does not have direct Roman origins. It is, however, reminiscent of Roman engineering and architectural styles. The bridge's purpose was to provide access to the castle and facilitate movement across the river, contributing to the strategic importance of the fortress.

As you stand upon the Bridge of Paderne, you can appreciate its simple yet sturdy design. The stone arches and sturdy structure stand as a testament to the craftsmanship of the time and the historical significance of the area. Take a moment to soak in the serene surroundings and imagine the footsteps of those who traversed this bridge centuries ago.

12:30pm – Drive to the Restaurant Veneza. It has many parking spots over there.

Image 8 - One of the dining places of the Restaurant Veneza

This restaurant has one of the best wine cellars in Portugal. Accompanied by traditional Portuguese dishes, this place is a definitely a must. The meal is around 20€, no drinks included. The wine menu is varied and extended, so the price list has a wide range, but you can find very high-quality wines at a perfectly accessible price.

Here is the link if you want to check out more information: Veneza Restaurant

15:00pm – Drive to the Marine. It has a parking lot nearby.

15:30pm – Head up to X-Ride stand (or any other cruise service you end up choosing). Get ready to embark on a truly memorable ride.

16:00pm – Get up on the boat and start your cruise.

This ride will take through the beautiful Algarve's coastline, passing by and stopping at beaches with peculiar rock formations, and luckily, be able to watch some dolphins.

Click on this link for more information on booking and services provided on the boat: Dolphin Watching and Caves Cruise - X-ride

Price: starting from 30€/person for a 2hour ride

18:30pm – Drive to the proximity of the Bullring and park there.

19:00pm – Walk around the Bullring and get to know that area. You are now in the New Town, with plenty of restaurants, shops, and fun things to do, see and buy.

Image 9 - Albufeira's Bullring

20:00pm – Walk up the street to the Restaurant Manel dos Frangos.

Image 10 - The famous "Frango da Guia."

Indulge in the mouthwatering delight of the "Frango da Guia," a succulent and flavorful grilled chicken dish. This signature dish is prepared to perfection, offering a blend of tender meat and delicious flavors that will surely satisfy your taste buds.

Enjoy a satisfying and fulfilling meal at Restaurant Manel dos Frangos, with prices typically averaging around 20€ per person, including drinks. This represents great value for a delectable dining experience that showcases the best of Albufeira's culinary traditions. Indulge in the flavors and ambiance of this local eatery, creating lasting memories of your visit to Albufeira.

22:00pm – Walk down the street and into the famous Strip

Image 11 - The Strip

The Strip is a vibrant and energetic road located in the New Town area of Albufeira. Known for its bustling atmosphere, this lively street is lined with numerous bars, bustling crowds, and eye-catching neon signs. It's a popular destination for party-goers from all around the world, offering a lively and vibrant nightlife experience.

As you explore the Strip, be prepared for an electrifying atmosphere where people gather to celebrate and have a good time. It's important to note that due to the lively nature of the Strip, it can get quite crowded and chaotic at times. Some revelers may engage in playful activities such as throwing beer, so be mindful of your surroundings.

When it comes to drinks, you'll find a range of options available at the bars along the Strip. Prices typically range from 5€ to 8€ per drink, offering a variety of alcoholic beverages to suit different preferences. Take your time to explore the various bars and discover the lively ambiance and diverse drink offerings that make the Strip a popular nightlife destination.

Enjoy the vibrant atmosphere of the Strip, soak up the energy, and embrace the lively party spirit that draws people from all over the world. 22:30pm – Have a drink at Lounge Bar Liberto's.

Image 12 - Liberto's Lounge Bar

Located amidst the vibrant and energetic atmosphere of the Strip, you'll find a sophisticated and refined lounge bar. This establishment offers a classy setting where you can relax, savor your drink, engage in conversation, and enjoy the ambient music that sets the mood. On certain evenings, they even host live shows, adding an extra touch of entertainment to your experience.

This lounge bar caters to those seeking a more laid-back and intimate ambiance. It provides a comfortable seating area where you can unwind and socialize with friends or loved ones. Additionally, for those who are inclined to dance, there is a designated dance floor where you can let loose and showcase your moves.

It's worth noting that the drinks at this upscale lounge bar are slightly more expensive, reflecting the premium quality and refined atmosphere. Indulge in the flavors of a perfectly crafted Gin & Tonic, available for approximately 10€. The attentive staff will ensure that your drink is expertly prepared, offering a delightful taste that complements the sophisticated atmosphere of the venue.

12:00am – Head to the Kiss club.

Image 13 - Kiss Club

Make your way to the Kiss club, a popular nightclub located nearby. It's important to note that upon arriving at around midnight, you may find the club to be relatively empty. In Portugal, it is customary for people to first enjoy the bars until they close around 4 am and then make their way to the clubs to continue the party until 7 or 8 am.

Embrace the local nightlife culture and be prepared for a gradual build-up of energy as the night progresses. While the club may be quiet when you arrive, rest assured that as the night unfolds, it will transform into a vibrant and bustling party scene.

Immerse yourself in the pulsating beats, energetic atmosphere, and lively dance floor as you dance the night away. Experience the unique charm of late-night clubbing in Portugal, where the festivities continue well into the early hours of the morning.

Please note that club closing times and party schedules may vary, so it's always a good idea to check the current operating hours and event listings for the Kiss club to ensure an optimal experience.

03:00am – Go back to the Bullring where you parked the car, and drive back to the hotel.

1st Day in Albufeira – Day Map

Below, you will find a map of all the suggested activities for your first day in Albufeira.

To ensure easy access and convenience, the map is provided in a user-friendly Google Maps format. Simply click on the photo or follow the link below to access the map. You can view it on any device, including tablets, laptops, and smartphones. Whether you're on the go or planning your itinerary in advance, this map will assist you in navigating the suggested activities seamlessly.

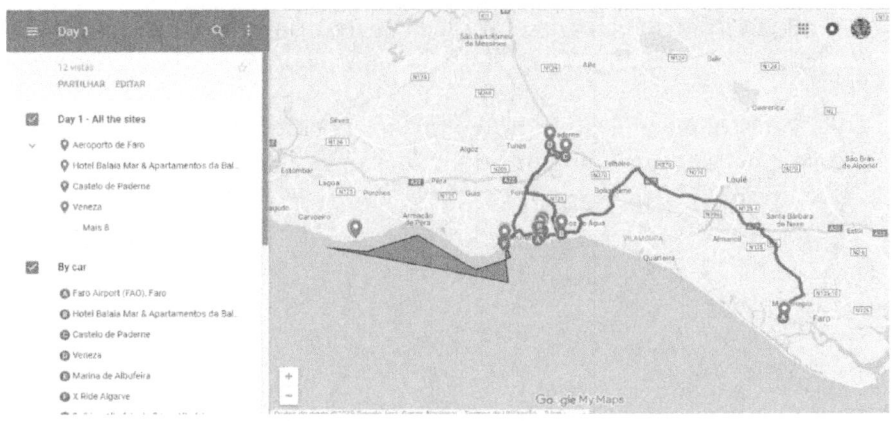

Get this Map Online in Google Maps Format: Day 1 Map

2nd Day in Albufeira

08:00 am - Rise and shine

Start your day bright and early, allowing yourself plenty of time to make the most of your second day in Albufeira.

09:00 am - Enjoy your breakfast at the hotel

Indulge in a delicious breakfast at your hotel. Whether it's a buffet spread or a freshly prepared meal, fuel up for the day ahead and savor the flavors that await.

10:00 am - Drive to Evaristo beach

Hop into your vehicle and set off on a scenic drive to Evaristo beach. This beautiful stretch of coastline offers crystal-clear waters, golden sands, and a tranquil atmosphere.

Enjoy a leisurely stroll along the shore, soak up the sun, and breathe in the refreshing sea breeze. Take a dip in the inviting waters or simply relax on the beach and embrace the natural beauty that surrounds you.

Evaristo beach is also known for its charming beachside restaurants, so consider indulging in a delicious seafood lunch while enjoying the stunning views.

Image 14 - Evaristo Beach

10:30am – Park near Evaristo beach, in the parking lot.

10:45am – Start your trip through the cliffs[4] and the beautiful Portuguese coastline. Just head forward, instead of left to the beach and restaurant. Head to the cliffs and keep going

---

[4]***Tip***: Don't forget to take a bottle of water, a hat, fresh and loose clothes, comfortable shoes, sunscreen and, of course, a camera, if you do this in the summer.

111

Image 15 - A beach with only that group in the peak of August

Embark on a captivating 2 to 2.5-hour hike along the scenic cliffs, and prepare yourself for a truly rewarding experience. As you traverse the rugged terrain, you'll be captivated by the breathtaking views that unfold before your eyes.

One of the highlights of this journey is the discovery of hidden gems, such as secluded beaches that are often unexplored by the masses. Despite the peak months of summer, these beaches retain a tranquil and almost deserted ambiance. Due to their exclusive access via the cliffs, many visitors, including tourists, are unaware of their existence or how to reach them.

As you navigate through the cliffs, you'll feel a sense of adventure and anticipation, knowing that you're about to uncover secret havens untouched by the bustling crowds. The journey itself becomes a rewarding experience, allowing you to immerse yourself in the beauty of nature and create lasting memories.

It's important to note that this hike requires a moderate level of physical fitness and comfortable walking shoes. Be sure to bring along water, sunscreen, and any other essentials to ensure your comfort during the excursion.

Take the road less traveled, and venture into the captivating realm of the cliffs. Discover hidden beaches and relish the tranquility that awaits, as you embrace the beauty of Albufeira's natural landscape in a truly unique and unforgettable way

1Image 16 - The sunset from the cliffs

Image 17 - The change in scenery

Prepare to be mesmerized by awe-inspiring views that will leave you breathless. Along your journey, you'll be treated to panoramic vistas that showcase the stunning beauty of Albufeira's coastal landscape. If you time your day accordingly, you can even plan to witness the magnificent sunset from one of the captivating locations along the way.

As you traverse the cliffs, you'll be treated to a remarkable transformation of scenery. At times, you'll be greeted by stretches of pristine, white sandy beaches that shimmer under the sun's rays. Other moments will unveil the majestic presence of red and orange cliffs, their hues contrasting against the deep blue of the sea. Some sandy patches may even resemble fine dirt or mud, adding a unique touch to the landscape.

Allow yourself to immerse in the ever-changing scenery, appreciating the diverse colors, textures, and natural formations that unfold before your eyes. Each turn and viewpoint will offer a new perspective, showcasing the raw beauty of Albufeira's coastal environment.

If you time your hike to coincide with the sunset, you'll be rewarded with a truly magical experience. Witness the sky ablaze with vibrant hues of orange, pink, and purple as the sun dips below the horizon, casting a golden glow over the cliffs and seascape. It's an unforgettable moment that will etch itself into your memory forever.

Prepare your camera to capture the awe-inspiring views and take a moment to appreciate the sheer beauty that surrounds you. Whether you choose to embark on this journey during the day or to catch the breathtaking sunset, be prepared to be swept away by the incredible scenery that awaits.

Image 19 - A beach of difficult access

But the best of all might be the very private beaches you will encounter. There are several small beaches along the coastline, which will enable you to be at a beach completely alone.

12:30pm – Have a drink at the Vila Joya Bar right on the cliff. The prices will be a bit high, considering the view! Then, make the same way back and have lunch at the trendy and fantastic beach restaurant, *O Evaristo*.

Indulge in a dining experience like no other at this restaurant with a prime location, where you can savor a delectable selection of fresh fish, seafood, and authentic Portuguese dishes. Embracing a unique concept, this popular establishment prides itself on not having a menu; instead, the knowledgeable waitstaff provide personalized recommendations tailored to each guest's preferences. Allow yourself to be guided through a culinary journey of flavors and surprises, as you trust in the expertise of the staff. With its exceptional reputation, this restaurant promises a memorable dining experience, with prices averaging around 40€ per meal (drinks not included).

For more information, click on this link: O Evaristo

15:30pm – Drive back to the center and park the car at the big parking lot at Parque Lúdico. From there, walk to the center and see all it has to offer.

The Old Town is absolutely beautiful. No need to make a perfect itinerary – the downtown is not that big, just lose yourself in it, go through the streets, to the highest points, enter the shops, and talk to the locals.

20:30pm – Have dinner at the beautiful restaurant *A Ruína*, meaning, in English, *The Ruin*.

Image 20 - The entrance of A Ruína

This famous restaurant is known for its fresh and delicious fish, but even more because of the terrific views it offers and the overall environment it brings to the table in a meal. It is built in a partially destroyed (by the earthquake of 1755) part of the Castle of Albufeira. The meal is around 30€, drinks included. For more info, click on this link: A Ruína

22:00pm – Nightlife in Albufeira is a truly remarkable experience.

Image 21 - Old Town, during the Winter

Roam around through the full streets of the Old Town. It has a little bit of everything. Bars for the older people and for the younger people. Places to sit down and talk, others just a dancefloor and loud music. You can find a British, Irish, Dutch, American, Portuguese, Italian restaurants on every corner.

Image 22 - The Tunnel

23:00pm – Go and visit the Shisha bar *A Casa do Cerro*. It is right by the parking lot where you left the car.

Image 23 - Comfortable seats at A Casa do Cerro

A more quiet and chill place, in A Casa do Cerro, you can have a drink, cocktail or tea, smoke a wide variety of flavored shisha and have a pleasant conversation, inside, sitting on very comfortable beds and chairs, or outside, feeling the cool breeze.

03:00am – Head back to the parking lot and return to the hotel.

2nd Day in Albufeira – Day Map

Below you can find the map with all the suggested places for your second day in Albufeira. You can click on the link to see it in the online format of Google maps so that you can easily navigate when you are in Albufeira.

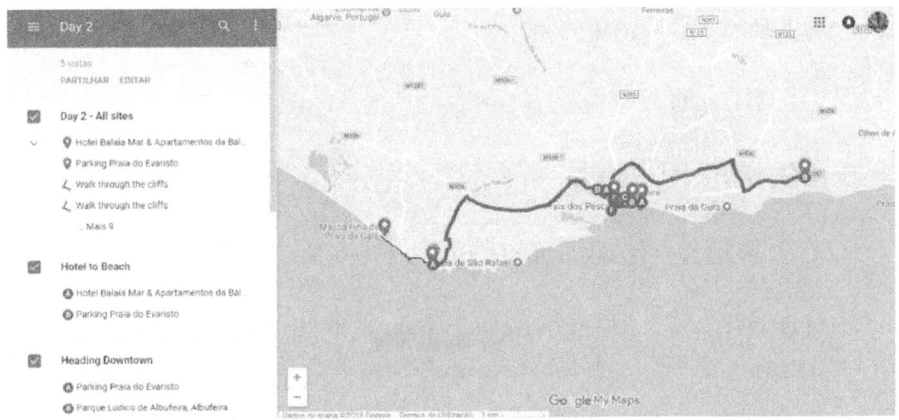

Get this Map Online in Google Maps Format: Day 2

3rd Day in Albufeira

08:00am – Wake up and pack your bags.

09:00am – Enjoy your last breakfast at your hotel.

09:30am – Check out of the hotel.

10:00am – Drive to Falésia Beach. There is a parking lot there. There will be signs indicating the pathway to the beach.

Image 24 - Praia da Falésia

Falésia Beach, aptly named for its stunning cliffs, is a truly remarkable destination. The breathtaking view of the vibrant red cliffs creates a mesmerizing contrast against the lush green pine groves that crown the dunes. The sand, soft and velvety, displays a mesmerizing blend of red and white tones, a result of the natural erosion of the cliff rocks. Stretching for nearly 7 kilometers (approximately 5 miles), this expansive beach seamlessly connects Albufeira to Vilamoura, a city situated to the east. With ample space to accommodate large crowds,

Falésia Beach becomes a sought-after haven during the peak months of summer. Its undeniable beauty has been recognized with numerous accolades, earning it prestigious awards at European and World competitions. Prepare to be captivated by the unparalleled allure of Falésia Beach as you soak up the sun, stroll along the shoreline, and immerse yourself in the breathtaking surroundings.

13:00pm – Lunch at the Yakuza Restaurant at the Sheraton Pine Cliffs Resort.

Image 25 - Yakuza Restaurant Entrance

Try this fusion cuisine restaurant presented by acclaimed cook Olivier. The concept is to mix the Japanese culture with the Mediterranean one. The result is absolutely fantastic. Plus, the view from the restaurant to the beach is stunning. It is also a great experience to go there just to watch the sunset and have a drink. The meal is around 35€/person, drinks included. Check out the website for the menu details and booking information.

Website: https://restaurantesolivier.com/en/yakuza/

15:30pm – Drive to *Zoomarine.*

Embark on an exciting adventure as you make your way to Zoomarine, a renowned marine park in Albufeira. Enjoy the convenience of a spacious parking lot located right by the entrance gates, ensuring a hassle-free experience.

Image 26 - The Dolphin's Show at Zoomarine

Zoomarine is water theme park, ranked the 7th best in Europe in its category. Perfect for families, it features several aquatic related shows with dolphins, sea-lions, and seals, as well as many other attractions. There are many activities for you to enjoy in this theme park. You should definitely wear sports or casual clothes, sun hat, comfortable shoes and sunblock.

The prices depend on the activities chosen, number of people, age, and some other factors. For full information on ticket prices, availability of group visits, discounts, activities and more, check out the website.

Website: https://www.zoomarine.pt/en/

20:15pm – Have dinner at the restaurant Ramires.

It was in this traditional restaurant that the original recipe was created, by the hands of the man Ramires himself. It is said to be the best *Franguinho da Guia* in the world. Now, you are able to compare it with the Guia Barbecue Chicken you had in the restaurant you were on the first day. Which one do you think is better?

In July and August, this restaurant does not accept reservations, so be there early, since it is a trendy place among locals and it might have a long waiting list, despite being a large restaurant. During the other months of the year, you can book a table online or call the number displayed on the website. The meal is around 25€/person, drinks included.

21:30pm – Drive to the Faro Airport.

22:10pm – Leave the car at the respective rental stand.

12:00am – Departure from Faro Airport.

3rd Day in Albufeira – Day Map

Below you can find the map with all the suggested places for your second day in Albufeira. You can click on the link to see it in the online format of Google maps so that you can easily navigate when you are in Albufeira.

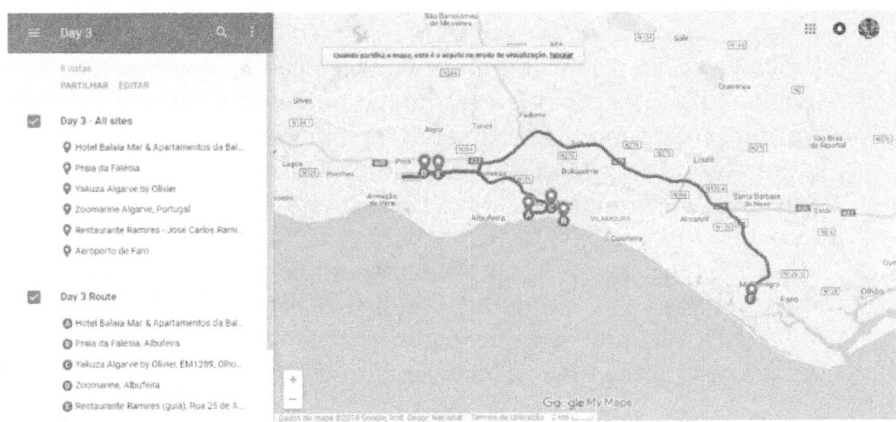

Get this Map Online in Google Maps Format: Day 3

Thank you!

As we conclude this travel guide to Albufeira, we hope that it has provided you with valuable insights, useful information, and inspiration for your upcoming visit to this beautiful destination. Albufeira offers a captivating blend of stunning beaches, rich history, vibrant nightlife, delicious cuisine, and warm hospitality, making it an ideal choice for travelers seeking a memorable experience.

From exploring the historical landmarks and soaking up the sun on the breathtaking beaches to indulging in the local cuisine and immersing yourself in the vibrant culture, Albufeira has something to offer every visitor. Whether you're seeking relaxation, adventure, or a mix of both, this coastal town is sure to exceed your expectations.

Remember to embrace the local customs, savor the flavors of Portuguese cuisine, and take the time to connect with the friendly locals who are always eager to share their love for their hometown. Whether you're strolling through the charming streets of the Old Town, dancing the night away on The Strip, or discovering the hidden gems along the cliffs, Albufeira invites you to create unforgettable memories.

As you plan your journey, we encourage you to refer back to this guide, utilize the provided resources, and tailor your itinerary to suit your interests and preferences. Keep in mind that Albufeira is a destination that evolves throughout the year, with each season offering its own unique charm and activities.

We wish you a remarkable adventure filled with joy, relaxation, and discovery as you explore the wonders of Albufeira. May your journey be filled with unforgettable experiences and leave you with cherished memories that will last a lifetime. Bon voyage!

Your friends at Guidora.

Printed in Great Britain
by Amazon